THE

Cutter's Practical Guide

TO

CUTTING AND MAKING

OVERCOATS

Bibliografische Information der Deutschen Nationalbibliothek:
Die Deutsche Nationalbibliothek verzeichnet diese Publikation
in der Deutschen Nationalbibliografie; detaillierte bibliografische
Daten sind im Internet über www.dnb.de abrufbar.

Reprint of the original from 1900
© 2025
Republished by Sven Jungclaus

Verlag:
BoD · Books on Demand GmbH, Überseering 33,
22297 Hamburg, bod@bod.de
Druck:
Libri Plureos GmbH, Friedensallee 273, 22763 Hamburg
ISBN: 978-3-7693-6697-6

OVERCOATS

IN ALL THEIR VARIED STYLES,

AND FOR ALL CLASSES

AND CONDITIONS OF MEN:

CIVILIAN, CLERICAL,

MILITARY & NAVAL, LIVERY, &c.

BEING

Part Five,

OF

THE CUTTERS' PRACTICAL GUIDE

TO THE CUTTING ALL KINDS OF GARMENTS.

BY W. D. F. VINCENT.

Author of " The Federation First Prize Essay on Trouser Cutting," &c., &c.

LONDON:

PRINTED AND PUBLISHED BY THE JOHN WILLIAMSON COMPANY LIMITED.

93 & 94 DRURY LANE, W.C.

"W.D.F. Vincent was born in Junie 1860 and began his career as an apprentice with Frederick Cooper in Yeovil. After completing his training, he briefly established his own businesses in Oxford and later in Maidenhead as a clothier and tailor, though neither venture was financially successful.

While in Maidenhead, Vincent won an essay competition on tailoring, which was open to all members of the National Federation of Foremen Tailors, titled "The Great National Work on Trouser Cutting, or Defects in Trousers." He submitted his entry under the pseudonym "Oxonian" and won the first prize. This success led him to secure a position with The Tailor and Cutter magazine. In the early years, Vincent contributed numerous articles on tailoring methods and techniques to the magazine. However, due to the terms of his employment, these articles were published without attribution to him.

By the 1890s, Vincent became a leading tailoring authority. His books, such as The Cutter's Practical Guide to the Cutting & Making of All Kinds of Trousers, became standard reference work. By 1917, Vincent referred to himself as a journalist. He died in June 1926.

The Tailor and Cutter magazine and academy were operated by John Williamson & Co Ltd. In the 1950s and 1960s, many tailors displayed their Tailor & Cutter Academy Diplomas, signed by W.D.F. Vincent, as the Chairman of Examiners, as a centerpiece in their shop windows. One such example can still be seen on display at the Museum of Welsh Life at St. Fagans in South Wales."

(cf. https://vincents.org.uk/family-history/w-d-f-vincent-tailor; 15.12.2024)

This edition is a reprint of the legendary *Cutter's Practical Guide* series; the first book was published in 1890. Although W. D. F. Vincent wrote many books on tailoring, these are the most popular. The entire text has been meticulously read, and the images have been carefully cleaned and edited to ensure the highest quality.

Part   1 – Juvenile Garments
Part   2 – Body Coats
Part   3 – Trousers, Breeches & Knickers
Part   4 – Livery Garments in all their varieties
Part 5 – Overcoats
Part   6 – Ladies' Garments
Part   7 – Defects, Remedies, Trying on
Part   8 – Economical Cutting
Part   9 – Lounges, Reefers, Norfolk, Sporting & Patrol Jackets
Part 10 – Waistcoats for Gentlemen, Ladies, Military & Naval Officers, etc.
Part 11 – Shirts, Undergarments, Collars, Cuffs, Aprons, etc.
Part 12 – Clerical Dress
Part 13 – British Military Uniforms

Content

AUTHOR'S PREFACE

We now introduce another instalment of our work — "The Cutters' Practical Guide", in which we are endeavouring to embody the result of experience, observation and careful study. Our emanations in this Series of works may not be perfect — we do not claim they are, but we have the satisfaction of knowing that they are — all of them — very helpful to very many Cutters, who bear willing testimony to the benefits they are deriving from their use.

We trust this work on Overgarments for all sorts and classes of men may be found equally useful to those who are treading the same pathway we have trod. We are earnestly desirous of helping such, by placing in their hands materials which will better fit them for the discharge of the duties devolving upon them in their different spheres. Thus we shall help in some measure to raise the status of our trade. Recent developments in the Art and Science of Cutting have rendered it possible to produce garments correct in fit and excellent in style.

This Art has, however to be acquired, and it is our ambition to contribute by this series of works, a medium by which this noblest of all Arts can be acquired. We trust as we doubt not, that the same success will attend this latest Part, as continues to attend the previous ones.

W. D. F. VINCENT.

PUBLISHER'S PREFACE

In previous Works issued from this office, Overcoats have been fully dealt with. But that was a number of years ago, and not only do fashions change, but systems and methods of production develop and improve. New ideas as to what constitutes good style, together with new and improved Systems of Cutting, are introduced as time proceeds. This being so, but a few years are necessary in order that most of such works may be termed old and out of date. This idea, we think, applies to the works on Overcoats we have previously published; hence this New Work which we have now the pleasure of introducing to the trade.

All the latest styles up to date, including the "Albert", which has been mostly confined to the Masher, or fashionable young gent, now promises to become a popular Overgarment. Every conceivable Overcoat, not for Civilians only, but Clerical, Naval, Military, Livery, &c., will be found set forth in these pages, in the form of beautifully illustrated Plates, each Plate showing all the details of the garment. This feature will be found a great acquisition by the Cutter. Our aim has been to produce a work thorough and complete, our patrons will judge how far we have succeeded. As a Cutting Guide and Instructor in everything pertaining to Overgarments, little remains, we think, that could be further desired. We have pleasure therefore in introducing this work to the many which have been issued from this office, and appreciated by Cutters throughout the world.

THE JOHN WILLIAMSON COMPANY LIMITED,

JOHN WILLIAMSON, *General Manager.*

"THE TAILOR AND CUTTER" Office,

93 & 94 Drury Lane, London, W.C..

PREVIOUSLY PRINTED BY THE JOHN WILLIAMSON COMPANY LIMITED,
93 & 94 DRURY LANE, LONDON, W.C.

https://www.becomeatailor.com

THE
CUTTER'S PRACTICAL GUIDE
TO THE
CUTTING AND MAKING ALL KINDS OF
OVERGARMENTS.

INTRODUCTION.

Amongst the many classes of garments to be found in Tailoring, Overcoats take a prominent place; for every trade, be it great or small, city or provincial, find at certain periods of the year fully one half of their trade in these garments. It is one of the most changeable branches of the gentlemen's trade, for we find greater revolutions in the style of over garments than in all other garments put together. Probably the fact that it is a special garment for a special season has something to do with that, and when gentlemen put their Overcoats away for the summer, they forget to make provision against moth, and so when they visit their wardrobe some chilly autumn evening, they find their Overcoat eaten in holes, and so a new coat for the next season has become inevitable. Or, it may be, one of the new styles takes his fancy, and as Overcoats are garments that require a little special adaptation to the times and seasons they are to be worn, it often happens that orders arrive in this way. The Overcoat that is suitable for walking, is quite a different garment to one intended for travelling or driving purposes. We also find those firms who cater for special classes of customers, introduce novelties specially adapted to the require-ments of their clients. As an instance, those firms whose trade lies chiefly amongst the medical profession, bring out a loose fitting D.B. Ulster with plenty of pockets, so that instruments and pocket cases can be easily carried about without inconvenience.

In the following pages we purpose treating of all the varieties as worn at the present time by gentlemen, giving such illustrations of novelties and specialities as will make the work valuable for reference in this go-ahead age. The practical details given are either the outcome of our own experience at the cutting board, or have been collected from the most reliable sources; whilst such specialities as the Military and Naval, are drawn from the sealed patterns deposited at the War and Admiralty Offices, as the standard styles of officers' Overcoats. We purpose dealing with these perhaps a little more fully than the demand for them may warrant, for the reason that there are many ideas to be found in these of an exceedingly practical and useful nature, for in their design practical utility has been more studied than appearance, and we doubt not but our readers will find them a great assistance in designing special garments of the Overcoat class.

We shall treat of the various styles of cutting Overcoats subsequently, and we will at once begin the practical part of our work by a description of

Measuring for Overcoats.

Here at the outset we find a difference of opinion existing among cutters. Ought the measures to be taken over the coat or over the vest? is a question often asked, and as there is something to be said on both sides, we will consider their respective claims briefly. It is quite true that being an over garment it should be cut in accordance with the size of the body and the garments it is worn over. It seems also a very common sense method to take the measures outside all that is to be worn under it; but if we do this it will only apply to the chest and waist, for unless we take the direct measures outside an Overcoat they will not be satisfactory, hence we prefer to take the measures quite in the ordinary way — the chest and waist measures over vest, and the direct measures over the ordinary coat. Our reasons for doing so are: 1st, The Overcoat is a garment desired to wear outside any under garment the customer may be wearing. 2nd, The measures so taken can be readily used for ordinary jackets or coats, should the customer favour you with an order for these. Still, it resolves itself practically into a matter of individual fancy as how the measures are taken. The general difference between a measure taken over the coat and one over the vest is two inches, so that whichever way they are taken, the cutter may with safety add that quantity or deduct it, if he wishes to vary the style in which the measure has been taken.

Those of our readers who have the former parts of this work will know we hold a very decided opinion on

The Advantages of Direct Measures.

The more we practice, the more this is confirmed, for by their aid the cutter is enabled to grasp the more important features of fit required in any garment for that particular customer. For example, the front shoulder and the depth of scye determine the balance required, so that, be the customer stooping or erect, these measures, if accurately taken, will give the relative length of back and front required. These two measures taken in conjunction with the over shoulder measure, decide the slope of the shoulder, so that, be the customer sloping-shouldered or short-necked, be he small in the shoulders or large, these measures will provide for all his peculiarities, and then if the across chest measures be taken to locate the front of the scye, the more important features of the pattern will be provided for in a way most suited to the requirements of that particular customer. It is sometimes argued that these measures are difficult to take, but we have not found them so, for with a very little practice and care we soon find the student is quite capable of taking them satisfactorily. The taking of measures is an operation that always requires care and attention, and the more careful the cutter is in this respect, the more successful he must be, for he must remember he has not only to fit the body, but also the head, and when he is taking the measures is an excellent opportunity of finding out his customer's wishes as to ease or closeness of fit, as well as many other details.

The Order of Measuring

Is as follows: First take the chest and waist, then the depth of scye from nape of neck, continue on to natural waist and full length; next the width of back with arm resting at side; then raise the arm at right angles to body, bring it forward, bend elbow, and continue the measure from centre of back to elbow and cuff, always considering your customer's taste on this matter. The across chest measure comes next, taken fairly easy from front of scye to front of scye; then follows the front shoulder, from nape of neck to bottom of scye in front, taken fairly close; and lastly, the over shoulder, taken from the depth of scye on the centre seam of back, over the shoulder to bottom of scye in front. Those for the 36 chest would probably read as follows: 36 chest, 32 waist, 9 depth of scye, 17 natural waist, 40 full length, 6¾ across back, 19 elbow, 32 full sleeve length, 8 across chest, 12½ front shoulder and 17 over shoulder.

Our reasons for taking the chest and waist measure first are that it gives you a clue as to what the other measures should be, so that when you find they vary from the normal, you may observe the reason for that variation. For example the depth of scye may be greater than proportionate, and you at once ask yourself: Is this customer stooping or long necked, and so your eyes get opened to defects that might otherwise pass unnoticed. We sometimes find cutters loud in their praises of

The Advantages of the Breast Measure System.

There is no doubt, under certain circumstances, it is the only method practicable. We here give the proportions these sectional measures bear in the normal figure to the breast measure. For the 36 breast it will be found that the depth of scye equals one fourth; the across chest at one inch less than a fourth; the front shoulder at one third plus half an inch, and the over shoulder at one inch less than a half. These divisions will enable the reader who prefers to work by the breast measure in lieu of the direct measures taken on each customer, to do so; but the developments of growth are such as to render these slightly erroneous in the large and very small sizes; as it is found the former are small in the shoulders and the latter are large as compared with these divisions of the breast, so that only one of the above four rules stand good in all cases, and that is the across chest, equally one inch less than a fourth, this only, varying for backward and forward shoulders, stooping and erect figures, &c. It will be fully understood these abnormalities always require special treatment when working by the breast measure system.

The following rule we have found to answer well for large and small sizes: For every inch above 36 deduct ¼ inch, and for every inch below, take of ⅛ inch; thus, for the 40, take off four quarters equalling one inch, making it 39; the fourth of this for the depth of scye would make it 9¾, the front shoulder at ⅓ plus ½ equals 13½ and the over shoulder at one inch less than half is 18½, and so on for the various sizes. Thus it will be seen, that whilst in the following pages we shall refer to these various quantities by their name, as the depth of scye, &c., the system can be worked either as a breast measure or direct measure method, the only variation being in the manner of fixing the amount of these.

The Requirements of an Overcoat

Are, that it shall fit over the ordinary underclothing, so that it is necessary it shall be larger in certain places only. These are a deeper scye, a wider back, a wider chest, a longer front balance, more spring over the hips, increased width from back seam to front edge, and a wider sleeve. In order to produce these variations, the following additions are made to. the measures: The natural waist length is increased ⅜, the width of back is increased ¼ inch, the across chest is increased ⅜, the front and over shoulder both ⅜, so that for the 36 size the across chest would be 8⅜, the front shoulder 12⅞, the over shoulder 17⅞ and so on. These additions do not provide for all the special requirements quoted above, but the remainder are arranged for in

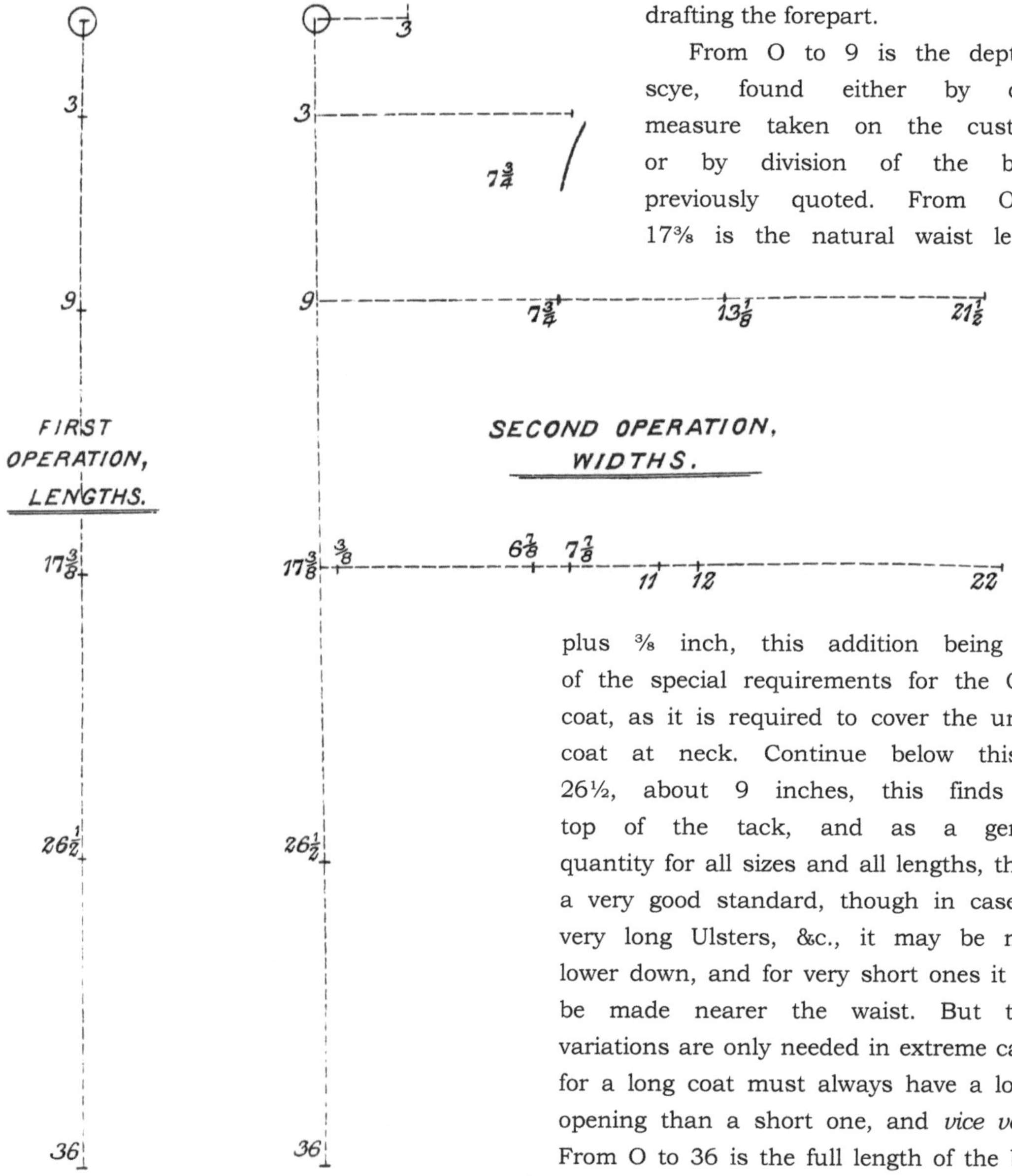

The System. First Operation: Points Of Length.

Begin by drawing a straight line as

shown on Diagram, and on this mark off from O to 3 one-third of the depth of scye, which, in this case, is 3 inches. The fixing of this point, however, is purely a matter of taste, and may be made higher or lower without in any way affecting the fit, because the back is measured when drafting the forepart.

From O to 9 is the depth of scye, found either by direct measure taken on the customer or by division of the breast previously quoted. From O to 17⅜ is the natural waist length,

plus ⅜ inch, this addition being one of the special requirements for the Overcoat, as it is required to cover the undercoat at neck. Continue below this to 26½, about 9 inches, this finds the top of the tack, and as a general quantity for all sizes and all lengths, this is a very good standard, though in cases of very long Ulsters, &c., it may be made lower down, and for very short ones it may be made nearer the waist. But these variations are only needed in extreme cases, for a long coat must always have a longer opening than a short one, and *vice versa*. From O to 36 is the full length of the back required, plus 2 seams (½ inch), and we are now ready to proceed with

The Second Operation: Points of Width,

Which consists in drawing lines at right angles to points O, 3, 9, and 17⅜, and on these marking off quantities as follows: From O to 3 is one-twelfth breast; a little, say 2 inches below point 3 mark off the width of back as taken direct on the customer, plus 3 seams (¾ inch), and curve the back outwards to line 3 on line 9; mark off from 9 to 21½ the half chest measure, plus 3½ inches. This added quantity varies for thick material; for heavy Naps, Friezes, &c., it should be increased to 4 or even 4½ inches, whilst for thin Venetians and summer Overcoatings, 2¾ or 3 inches will be found sufficient, so that the amount added to the half chest measure must be fixed by judgment at the time of cutting, carefully considering the thickness of material and the desired ease in the garment. Having fixed point 21½ we measure back from this the across chest measure plus ⅜ inch, the across chest measure being fixed either by taking it direct on the customer or by the division of the breast, but always adding ⅜ for the

Overcoat. On line 17⅜, mark off to ⅜, ⅜ of an inch; from construction line to 6⅞ is one sixth breast, plus ⅞ inch, on to 7⅞ is one inch more, and continuing on to 11 and 12 is respectively 4 and 5 inches beyond 6⅞ and 7⅞. Now measure up from ⅜ to 6⅞, add that to 7⅞, but omitting the intervening space, and measure on to 11; take that on to 12, omitting the space between 11 and 12, and from 12 measure across to 22 the half waist measure, plus 3½ inches; this amounts to ⅜ to 6⅞ plus 7⅞, to 11 plus 12, to 22 equals the half waist, plus 3½ inches. Having thus fixed the points of width, we proceed with the

Third Operation: Points of Form.

From 3 come up to ¾, three quarters of an inch always and connect ¾ with O by a gradual curve, and so shape the back neck; from ¾ past point W the shoulder is drawn and the back scye is formed, and the side seam is drawn by a curve through 7¾, or depth of scye line, to 6⅞ on waist line, and below that it is continued straight. The back seam is drawn from O to ⅜, and ⅜ to 26½, and in order to get the run of the back tack come out from 26½ one inch and draw a line from O through this point 1 to bottom, this completing the back, with the exception of bottom, which is square across from back construction line. We now proceed to get the points D and F for the

THIRD OPERATION,
FORM.

front shoulder. First measure from O to ¾ of the back, and deduct that from the front shoulder measure plus ⅜, thus front shoulder 12½ plus ⅜ because it is an Overcoat equals 12⅞ minus the back neck leaves 9⅞ for the first segment, to be made from point 13⅛ in the direction indicated by 1 and 2 at F; now add 1 inch to this, making it 10⅞, and by this sweep as indicated at 3 4, the pivot being changed in this instance to 21½, thus making the point F where the segments cross each other, 1 inch further from 21½ than it is from 13⅛. Point F indicates the neck point of the front shoulder, the scye end being found by measuring from 9 to W, and deducting that quantity from the over

as the amount by which to sweep for the third segment at 5, 6, D. In doing this the tape should be put at 13⅛ and the finger put on the tape 1½ inches above that point before sweeping, so that the measure may be applied in the same way that it is taken. We now pass on to the

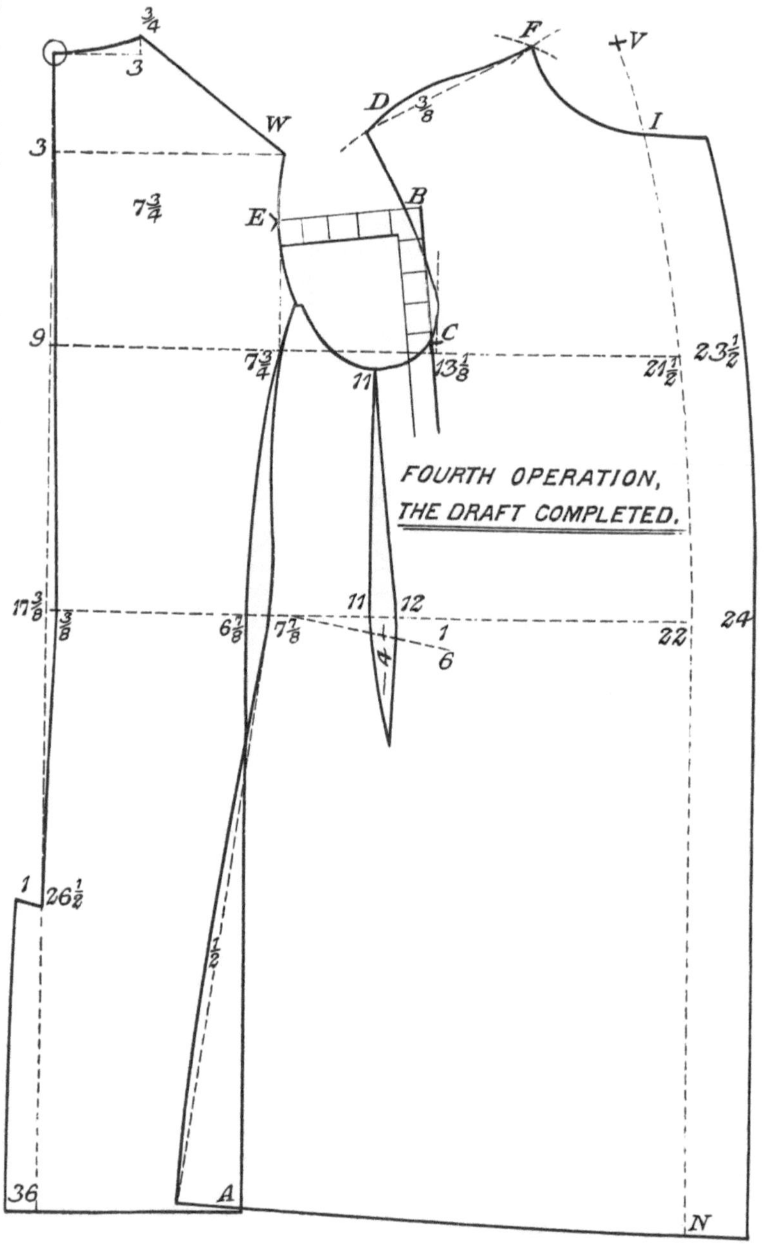

Fourth Operation. The Draft completed:

Shape the shoulder from F to D by drawing a straight line and adding ⅜ of round as illustrated, the width from F to D being made ¼ inch narrower than the back. Now proceed to draft the scye, keeping it as hollow as possible consistent with a curve at 13⅛; take the bottom of scye ½ an inch below the depth of

shoulder measure plus ⅜, and sweeping by the remainder from point 13⅛, thus 9 to W equals 9½ the front shoulder 17, and with the ⅜ added, for its being an overcoat makes 17⅜, and that quantity minus 9½ leaves 7⅞ scye line, bringing it up the back to meet the scye of back. Now form the sideseam by letting the forepart touch the back down to 7¾ and keeping it fairly flat down to 7⅞, below which it is sprung out by drawing a line at right angles to 7⅞ — 6, point 6 being six inches in from side seam and down one inch; beyond this line ½ inch of round is added as per diagram. Now draft the fish under the seam, starting at 11 on depth of scye line to 11 and 12 on the waist line, and terminating it at four inches below the waist line. Next proceed to the front; from F to V is ⅟₁₂ breast, and I is the same amount below V, gauging the level of V by F O parallel to line 9 21½. From V draft the breast line through 21½, 22 to N, and beyond this allow the button stand or overlap, which for a fly front is fixed 2 inches. The run of the button is found by measuring from 22 to N three quarters of an inch more than 6⅞ to A, thus forming a slight curve. Of the shape of the lapel, the position of the pockets, and many other details we shall have something to say when treating of the various styles, so we proceed to deal with the sleeve.

Fifth Operation.

One of the most important phases of cutting all kinds of garments is the harmony of parts, and possibly there is no part of a garment in which this more imperative than in the sleeve and the scye. There is a certain amount of latitude allowed in the position of the seams, so that a narrow back can be compensated for by a larger sleeve head and a longer hind arm, hence one of the first things we have to consider in cutting a sleeve is the harmony of these two parts, and as the scye is the first to be drafted we measure it in order to get the sleeve the proper form to fit it. So after we have drawn our lines at right angles as illustrated on this diagram, we proceed to get point 13⅛ by measuring the width of the scye of the coat as illustrated from 7¾ to 13⅛, and making 7¾ and 13⅛ of the sleeve the same distance apart that those

points are on the body. Point 7¾ does not necessarily come on the side seam, but must always be found by squaring up from the depth of scye line 9, 21½ to the most backward point of scye, illustrated on the draft by E. The next point we have to study is the balance of the sleeve, which must be done in harmony with the customer's requirements, as well as the scye, and in order to do this we place the square with either arm resting against the pitches E C. A very good plan is to stick a pin in either of these points upright, and then the square can be easily turned about till the arm extending towards the pocket is resting in the position deemed the most useful for the particular customer we are dealing with. A very good guide in this respect is to let it come over the centre of the pocket flap. As soon as we have this arranged, we proceed with the

Sixth Operation: The Sleeve Head,

And mark up from B to C the same amount there is from the angle of the square at B to the fore arm pitch as it rests in the scye, so that the hang of the sleeve can be easily arranged in harmony with our customer's form and business. The erect man requires a backward hanging sleeve as also does the bath-chair man, whilst for stooping figures and those whose occupation bring their arms forward, as a coachman, a forward hang is needed. To get the size of the sleeve head, measure from E to W of the scye and add that to D and measure across to C, so that C E of the sleeve agrees with C E of the scye with the shoulder closed, the measure being taken straight across and not round the scye. Point ½ is found midway between the points C E, and a line drawn from B to ½ forms a good guide for the round of sleeve head, a good average amount of round being produced by adding on ¾ inch midway between ½ and, D. Strictly speaking this should agree with the hollow of shoulder between D C, and if a line is drawn straight from D C of the front shoulder, and a measure taken from the middle of the straight line to the scye, this will give the accurate amount of round demanded. The sleeve head now being complete we proceed to mark off the length, &c., as illustrated on the

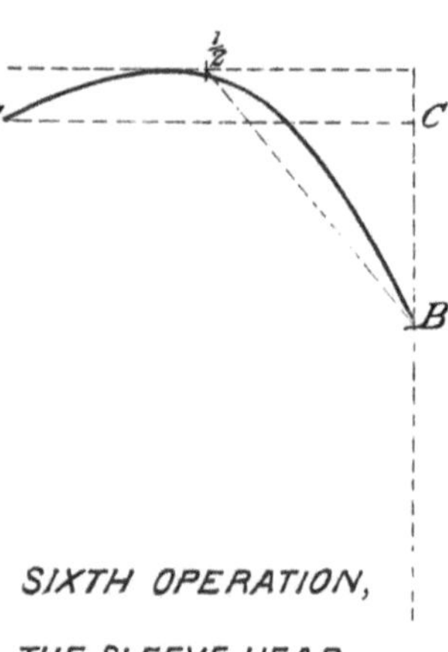

Seventh Operation: The Sleeve Complete.

First of all measure the width of back across to E, deduct ¾ inch from it for the seams consumed, one in the back and two in the scye, and apply that as L E, continuing on to N, the length to the elbow and T to the cuff, plus say ½ inch, as it is generally desirable to get the overcoat sleeve to fully cover the under coat sleeve. Having got the position of the elbow and cuff, mark off the width to taste, hollowing the fore arm at G 1 inch. A very good guide for the width of the elbow from G to N is one-fourth breast minus half an inch, and for the cuff from T to H at one-sixth breast plus one inch. The run of the cuff may be got either by sweeping from T by E or by squaring from N T. The hind-arm is slightly rounded between N and T, and slightly hollowed between N E.

It only now remains to form the under sleeve, which is done by measuring *round* the lower part of scye between the two pitches, as from E 11 to C, and whatever that measures apply from 1 to 2 of the sleeve. Make a pivot of N and sweep from E to 2 and hollow the underside sleeve as shown and complete by drawing the hind arm from 2 to N.

We now have a complete system for the sleeve and body, but as the system is merely the foundation we shall illustrate how it is applied to the various types of garments as we proceed. A careful study of these first pages will simplify what is to follow, and make the production of every kind of Overcoat a matter of the greatest simplicity, so that we shall be able to devote our remarks to a few practical details and observations of the difficulties to be overcome.

The Trimming.

In trimming, the purpose for which the garment is required must be borne in mind. Having, for instance, to go over another garment, the sleeve linings should slip easily. The best sleeve linings are undoubtedly satin, and as this can be got now fairly cheap — 2/3 to 2/6 a yard — this would only add 4/- or 5/- to the price of a coat. If this should be an objection, the new make of Glissade makes an excellent substitute, so much so, that it is far preferable to Italian cloth, but if this latter material be used see that it is cut from the width of the material and not from the length. Whatever the sleeve lining is made from, it should be firmly flash-basted to the seams, otherwise the continual strain of putting on will prove too much for the felling of sleeve head. If the body lining is of woollen plaid, it should be thoroughly shrunk before being used, and even then it should be left loose at the bottom, or a facing of the same material as the body of the coat put all round the bottom, a plait left in the length of the lining and pressed over so as to allow a little latitude for shrinking. There are various methods of securing the forepart facing to the lining. One is to seam it on, another is to slate the facing on the top of the lining, and stitch it raw edge, sometimes "gimping" the edge out nicely. Another method is to bind the edge with a bit of Satin or Satin ribbon and then lap it on the lining.

Manipulating the Seams.

In sewing the seams, the only one that requires special attention is the shoulder, as the straight hang of the present style of Chester does away with any necessity of stretching or shrinking the sides. The gorge should be slightly stretched, starting 1 inch from the neck point; the shoulder should be strained up also about 1 inch from neck point, and the scye stretched about 2 inches from the shoulder end. The back should be held on to the forepart at about 2 inches from shoulder, but only slightly. A ply of tweed may be secured to the facing, either by rows of stitching or flash-basting, to give a firmness to the shoulder. A small three-cornered pad made of three plies of canvas, nicely graded from about 3 or 4 inches at the sides, will facilitate the fit just at the shoulder ends, and remove that droop that naturally exists just at the end of the shoulders. The facings of shoulder should always be put in wider than the outside, for it must be borne in mind that the shoulder is hollow, and if we are to produce a satisfactory fit, we must work it up accordingly.

Working up the Fronts.

In working up the fronts of Chesterfields, it is a mistake to draw in the edges very much, indeed beyond a very trifle just over the breast, they should only be steadied, so as to prevent their stretching; for being exposed to all sorts of weather, any extra amount of drawing in would soon show itself in a most objectionable manner. If the garment is for a corpulent figure it is far better to take a V out of pocket mouth and up under the arm than to cut a very round front edge. This is illustrated in "The Cutters' Practical Guide to the use of Model Patterns", price £ 2/6, from our Office. For dealing with corpulent figures this is one of the best arts in the trade, getting rid as it does of the superfluous drapery without either cutting a very round edge, or resorting to manipulation of the front edge to the extent which is likely to produce unsatisfactory results after a little wear.

Putting in the Pockets.

In putting in the pockets, the stays should be carried either into the scye or up into the sideseams; and see that they are arranged as stays, not, as we have seen some, with the linen on the bias. A pocket stay is put as a support to the pocket, and to relieve the strain on the pocket ends where the material is weakest. The bottom edge of the pocket should have stay tape put along and brought up round the end of the mouth, as well as the linen. A facing should be put to the pocket mouth, certainly on the bottom edge, and if not le behind the flap, then put corner pieces so as to prevent any possibility of the pockets showing through. The hip pockets of a Chesterfield should always be of woollen material, or chamois leather; the latter if good, makes an excellent pocket, but not better than the woollen plaid, and as there are generally pieces left out of the lining, when this is used, it is naturally used most frequently. It is a mistake to put Chesterfield pockets in of cotton or linen, for to put the hand in such a pocket on a bitter cold day is anything but pleasant; with the wool pocket it is a comfort. In tacking the pockets do not use a private tack, as it is very apt to cut the cloth; the bar tack is not only stronger but preferable in the other respect also. We prefer working these with twist as it preserves its colour better than the ordinary sewing silk. Thin cloth forms the best flap linings for Chesterfields, and this should be put in slightly smaller to make the flap curl inwards. A

piece of linen should be put down the canvas, where the buttons are to stand, and in sewing on the buttons see that they are put on with a good shank, and have every button tacked behind, as it greatly supports the button and does away with the likelihood of its tearing away.

The Collar.

The collar should be cut with plenty of fall edge, and any stretching that is necessary should be done to the stand part, for the fall being the part exposed to the moisture of the atmosphere, it will soon return to its natural shape if its form has been produced by the workmen's muscles and the heat of the goose. It is very important to have a close fit at the crease edge, and this is best secured by inserting a good bridle along the crease of turn. This should be a strip of linen and it must be cut on the straight, if on the selvage all the better, and not less than one inch wide. The length along the fall edge is very easily infused in the cut by letting this part partake of a round rather than a straight; this is the more important when it is borne in mind that Chesterfields more than any other garment are worn buttoned up to the throat, which requires a considerable length of leaf edge if it is to fit nicely.

Sewing in the Sleeves.

In putting in the sleeves, it will be well to notice the amount of fulness there is in the sleeve head, and if there is much and the material is of an unshrinkable character, such as Beavers, Meltons, &c., then it will be advisable to put in a drawing thread to draw it in the necessary amount and shrink the fulness away before it is sewn into the scye. The fulness of sleeve head should commence at 1 inch from shoulder seam, and reach the greatest amount of fulness about 4 inches from the shoulder seam and then continue gradually down to the forearm pitch. If there is any fulness in the underside, put it in a pleat just at the very bottom of the scye, always keeping the undersleeve in tight just round the back scye; a drawing thread put round the back scye for 4 or 5 inches and drawn in slightly will facilitate the fit at this critical part; and in order to prevent it stretching in the opening of the scye seam, some sew a piece of silk selvage in with the seam, which is a very good plan.

Making up the Fly.

The fly frequently causes a lot of trouble, especially just under the turn, where there always appears a pulpiness. Many are the remedies suggested, and they nearly all have their effect in the right direction, but we have not yet seen a fly-front Chesterfield that has not had this defect after a little wear. It has been all right whilst the cutter's hand has been there to put it right and smooth the fulness away, but wait till it has been worn a little, and there it is, all alive. Some attribute it to using fly linings that shrink; there can be no doubt that whatever is used for this purpose would be best passed under the damp rag and iron, to prevent any possibility of after contraction. Some, again, have attributed it to an insufficient length and width of facing at that part, and there is something in this also; it is astonishing the extra material required in the facing at this part to what is required for the outside, so our advice is put plenty of facing just over the turn. Some have carried the canvas through the fly instead of the forepart; others leave the fly open a good inch above the turn and across the top of the fly.

In stitching in the fly, do not stitch through facings and all, it gives a sloppy appearance. Another point to remember is to keep the fly a trifle — say a seam — behind the edge of the forepart, and before sending it home see that the fly is tacked between the button holes.

The Back Tack.

The only other point it is necessary to notice is the back tack. This looks best when the slit is made to form a continuation of the back seam, and the tack itself put in neatly in a slanting direction, the lining being so arranged at this part, as for the back seam to appear continuous. In this opening a hole is sometimes inserted after the manner of a blind fly, but of course this is only when the garment is somewhat long.

OVERCOATS

IN THEIR VARIOUS STYLES.

FLY FRONT CHESTERFIELD.
Plate 1.

Now that we have explained the working of the system generally to all kinds of Overcoats, we will take each one separately and treat of its special features. The first of these will be the Fly Front Chesterfield, that being the style most largely used for Summer and Winter, Spring and Autumn. It is the popular Overcoat, especially with those who do not care to adopt special styles as they are introduced. It is un-doubtedly. one of the neatest and least obtrusive. It varies in length as well as the degrees of closeness in which it is worn at the waist. The style illustrated on Plate 1 is what may be termed the medium style, though the length is not taken down to the full extent, which would average from 38 to 40 for a figure of 5 feet 9 inches. Beyond that length we should consider it long, and shorter than that we should regard as short.

The Materials

Used for Chesterfields of this class vary considerably, and as the nature and sub-stance differ, so alterations must be made from the quantities given on Diagram. For Summer wear, Venetians, Worsteds, and Vicunas are largely used, and for these it will not be necessary to allow so much for making up by fully half an inch, they being thin and of a workable nature. These materials are more generally made up with the ordinary S.B. turn, as illustrated on Plate 3, and when silk is used to line or face them, it is often brought right to the edge. The style of lapel illustrated on this diagram is more popular for winter materials and heavier garments. Such are mostly made from Beaver, Melton, Nap, and kindred materials, the edge being varied accordingly. The Melton, for example, would probably be double stitched on the raw edge if of a good quality. The Beaver might be treated in the same way, or stoated and stitched in the style illustrated on the Diagram. They look very nice in a style of edge frequently adopted — piped with either cloth or velvet, care being taken to make all parts in harmony. The Naps and such goods are more generally stoated and stitched, though the piping is frequently used for them. The principal points to be observed in cutting from the stand point of material is, that the thinner the cloth the less is required for making up, and rather less overlap allowed, as the thin goods do not make up such a bold front as the heavier goods.

The average length required would be 2 to 2¼ yards.

The Position of the Pockets

Is not always correctly fixed. To assist our patrons in this matter we give the following guides: If the waist line is taken as a guide, place the top of the flap at about 4½ inches below it; or if the sleeve is taken as the guide, then place the forearm at the forearm pitch and mark the flaps to come on the level of the cuff. Some cutters take direct measures to guide them in this,

whilst others leave it till trying on to mark the exact position. Either of the two first will prove satisfactory in the majority of cases, especially if the one is used to check the other, and, in case of any difference, going half-way between the two. Place the pocket a trifle nearer the sideseam than the breast line, and make the pocket flaps on hips about 7 inches long by 2½ wide. The ticket pocket is placed a little in front of the hip pocket, and is put on the waist line, the size of flaps being about 3½ by 1¾. The breast pocket is placed so that the bottom of welt comes on a level with the scye, and running down about 1 inch at the front. The size of the welt would be 5½ by ⅞; or, if a flap, then 5½ by 2. Sometimes the ticket pocket is put in the facing of the left forepart, so as to be out of sight. The hip pockets should always be woollen, but we shall refer to that later on. We will now proceed to give a few

Practical Details.

The fly should extend about 7 inches below the waist line, though some few firms carry the stitching right through to the bottom. With 2 inches allowed beyond the breast line, the buttons should stand nearly 3 inches from the edge, and the forepart tacked through to keep them firm, as there is frequently a good strain on these buttons. Our Diagram shows a velvet collar, and in connection with this we would point out that it is not considered good taste to put on both silk facings and a velvet collar, as these being features intended for ornamentation, to put on both over do it. It will be noticed there is no stitching round the bottom, this being omitted with the idea of preventing any apparent shortening tendency, as a line formed by stitching or with binding would do.

When a facing is put round the bottom to fell the lining to (a style much favoured by some firms in order to prevent any dropping of the lining below the bottom edge) and the facing is not simply a piece turned up, but is a separate piece put on, then it would be advisable to stitch it in the same style as the edge to keep it firm. But the cutter's aim should be as a rule to avoid any and everything that shortens the apparent height of a customer, it being generally acknowledged that lines formed round the body have that effect, and are consequently undesirable.

D.B. CHESTERFIELD WITH WHOLE BACK. Plate 2.

During recent years there has been no variation from the standard style of Fly Front Chesterfield that has become more popular than the Double Breasted Overcoat with a whole back. These variations being amongst the most important from the standpoint of style, we have selected them to form the subject of a Diagram Plate with description. Although we illustrate both these variations on this page, they do not, of necessity go together, although the whole back is very frequently associated with the D.B. Chester. In cutting

Whole Back Chesters.

The variation made depends to a large extent on the closeness or looseness of the fit. In its simplest form, when the garment is intended to fit with the ordinary degree of closeness, all that is necessary is to omit the suppression at natural waist, and place the centre of back on the construction line, arranging a trifle extra spring at the sideseam. In this style, if the garment is cut long it will be found necessary to have slits at the sides, varying in length according to the length of the coat, otherwise it will contract about the bottom as the legs are extended when walking. In making up this style it will be found an advantage to shrink the back, but we do not think the crease down the centre is the best place for this. The proper place to shrink the back is about 2½ inches on either side of centre, just about the place where the sideseam of a body coat would come, as that fits into the hollow under the blades, which is always the most pronounced depression in the back. This method also divides the back into three equal parts, and allows form to be infused into the back far easier than when it is only done in the centre. There are many garments cut with a whole back that are not intended to fit close. Then the style of cutting the back varies; the safest rule that can be given is to come out beyond the construction line at the back half the amount that is added at the sides, so that if the forepart overlaps the back 1 inch at sideseams instead of being suppressed that amount, then the centre of back should be drawn by coming out from 17⅜ 1 inch, and drawing the centre of back quite straight through it. Some may think a line drawn angularly will not be suitable for placing on the crease, but a little investigation will soon show that any back with the centre cut *straight* can be placed on the crease edge, no matter how it is drawn on the draft.

Double Breasted

Garments are very easily produced by merely adding an extra quantity of overlap beyond the breast lines. But simple as this is there is still plenty of scope for taste and style. The amount allowed beyond the breast line in the draft is 3 inches, that being a good medium amount; there is seldom less allowed than 2½ or more than 4½ inches, and it must always be borne in mind that the quantity of overlap allowed influences the position of the buttons, the buttons standing as far behind the breast

line as the eye of the hole is in front of it; so that when a small amount, such as 2½ inches is allowed on the front, the buttons would stand closer together, whilst if 4½ was added, there would be a greater distance between the rows of buttons. In shaping the lapel it should always be remembered it is formed for style only, and though it may be required to button up to the throat occasionally, yet that is the exception rather than the rule. In the draft the lapel commences to point upward about 1 inch from the breast line V I and the end of the gorge at I is kept straight, these being

Features of Style

That are well worthy of study. It should always be the aim of the cutter to get the drawing seam of his collar to run nearly parallel to the fall edge, that giving an appearance that is generally approved — indeed so much is this so, that sometimes when silk facings are used, the silk is brought higher than the drawing seam in order to produce this effect. On double breasted garments the silk facings are generally brought to the ends of the holes, and extend to midway between the second and third hole; this is when it is applied for ornamentation only, and of course does not apply to the case where the foreparts are lined through with it. Some cutters take a V out of the lapel at I, but this we do not usually do for Overcoats, as it has a tendency to shorten the outside edge of the lapel. It is, however, useful when a long front edge has been cut. Overcoats made in the style illustrated frequently have the seams either slated or raised, and in doing this it will be necessary for the cutter to leave inlays on the part that is going under; thus the back would overlap the forepart at both sideseam and shoulder, so that inlays will be necessary round the shoulder and down the sideseam of fore-part. If no inlay has been left on a piece can be serged to take its place, but that means trouble that might easily be avoided by a little thought on the cutter's part when cutting out.

GENTS' COVERT COAT.
Plate 3.

The Covert Coat is undoubtedly the over-garment best suited for Spring and Summer wear; for riding and walking nothing is better, the material from which they are made, more generally being a Venetian which has now become so associated with Covert Coats that many always list it as Covert Coatings. Venetian, however, is not the only material; Meltons and Beavers, as well as Tweeds to imitate Venetian, have all been used for these garments, the latter being used for cheap garments and the former for the warmer Winter coats.

The Special Features

Of the Covert Coat are as follows: It is a smart close-fitting Overcoat cut to come about 3 inches over a Lounge. It has no vent in the back but one is placed on either side about 4 inches deep. It is made fairly close fitting in the body, is finished fly front, generally has 4 out pockets, viz., 2 on hips, ticket pocket and breast pocket; the latter being sometimes finished with a welt. The seams are seldom left plain, the more general plan being to strap them about ⅝ or ¾ wide with the same material as the coat, but cut the cross way of the pile so that the pile on these would run round the body instead of up and down. The seams, however, are not always finished in this way; they are often simply raised as in our Diagram. Some-times they are raised and double stitched, whilst for Meltons and such material they

are more frequently slated and double stitched, the edges being finished to match the seams. The sleeves are for the most part finished with five rows of sewing round the cuff, and in the event of the seams being strapped the strappings of the hind-arm is sometimes made to form one con-tinuous run from the shoulder seam. When this is done a little variation must be made in cutting, bringing the shoulder seam of back a little lower and also cutting a some-what narrow topside sleeve. As regards the cutting, the Covert Coat is cut very much the same as an ordinary Overcoat, the only variation being when thin material is used there should only be 2¾ or 3 inches allowed beyond the half breast measure. The fronts are invariably finished with a fly, the amount of overlap left is 2 inches, the mode of doing this being fully shown in the Diagram.

Hints on Making.

It is a very good plan to leave a turn up round the bottom to fell the lining on to, and if the lining is wool, it is very important it should be thoroughly shrunk before being used, otherwise the first shower the coat is exposed to will cause the lining to shrink and produce a very bad effect, which can only be rectified by making use of the turn up suggested. When the seams are strapped the strapping is cut double the width it is desired, the edges serged together and then pressed flat. The seams are sewn and pressed open in the usual way, and then the strapping is laid on and stitched on either side. It is not always an easy matter to strap the forearm seam of the sleeve unless a machine with a long narrow arm is used, and few machines are made that way now. The easiest way of getting over that difficulty is to strap the hindarm in the usual way before seaming up the fore-arm seam, then mark on the topside where the edge of the strapping should come, and then stitching it on before the seam is sewn, after which the seam is sewn, the strapping having been previously stitched on the other edge. After the forearm seam is sewn the strapping can then be felled to the underside at the forearm, and the wearer will seldom know the difference. There are a few

Practical Details

That will be of service to the inexperienced cutter when dealing with these garments. Covert Coats are sometimes made up with no other pockets than a breast pocket. A tab is put under the collar on the left side, a button being put under the right collar end, to permit of its being buttoned over, the size of this would be 3½ by 1½ or 1¾, an eyelet hole in one end, and a button hole in the other. The tab and the flaps are all lined with the same cloth for preference, though Italian cloth is sometimes used for the latter, but it does not make as good a finish as the cloth lining.

Waterproofing.

These garments are intended to keep out a good shower. Many of the woollen houses supply the cloth waterproofed, or will get it waterproofed for their customers at a short notice. If our readers should desire to do this themselves we give the following receipt:

Take 4 ounces of powdered alum and 4½ ounces of sugar of lead, and dissolve in 3 gallons of water, stirring it twice a day for two days. When this is quite clear, and any sediment sunk to the bottom, pour off the clear part and add 2 drachms of isinglass that has been previously dissolved in warm water, and mix together. Steep the cloth in this for six hours, and then hang it up to drain dry, as wringing must be avoided. This is simple and efficacious, and is by no means expensive, and if due care is taken to keep the sediment out, and to use clean water, no stain will result.

CHESTERFIELD FOR CORPULENT FIGURE. Plate 4.

The corpulent figure is not one of the easiest to fit with a Chesterfield, owing to the falling away of the figure directly below the prominence of the stomach; that being the largest part of the body, all that is necessary is that it shall hang straight down from that part. There are two methods of making the necessary provision to avoid superfluous material in the skirt — for that is the real difficulty, and one which, if not removed, will show itself in decided petticoat folds from the front downwards.

The old style of meeting this, was to cut the front away below the waist, as indicated by line H, adding on the usual overlap anc then well working up the fronts, so that the round is brought back to a *straight* line, and the fulness so produced well worked away over the stomach, &c. In a coat for a very corpulent figure this round would be so excessive that to do the necessary manipulation would be found a difficult matter, especially in some materials. But, even when done and nicely pressed away, the fact remains, and the cutter knows it, that the first shower of rain will leave the edge all puckered and drawn, and in anything but a satisfactory condition; so that whilst this plan answers all right as far as finishing the garment is concerned, if proper manipulation is put into it, still seeing that Chesterfields are garments that are intended to be worn in all kinds of weather, and that any moisture will spoil its appearance; if that depends on the iron, this method can hardly be considered a success. Something better must therefore be discovered, and the most successful is an adaptation of the principle so generally applied to

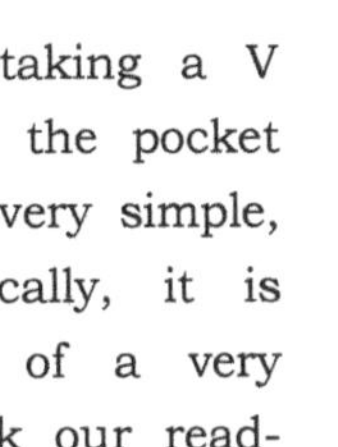

large vests, and consists of taking a V out from the sideseam across the pocket mouth. Although this appears very simple, if it is not done systematically, it is likely to produce difficulties of a very annoying kind; hence we think our readers will find the following plan of treatment will be both simple and useful. The first thing that is necessary for us to define is: What constitutes

Disproportion at the Waist.

The reply must be found in understanding what constitutes proportion, and then any variation from it will give us disproportion. There are some authors who have fixed the proportionate waist at one-sixth less than the chest, such as 36 chest, and 30 waist; 42 chest and 35 waist, and so on, but we do not find this plan in harmony with our experience. The best plan we have yet found is to take four inches from the chest measure in all sizes, and then taking that as the standard of proportion — thus: 36 chest, 32 waist; 40 chest, 36 waist, and so on. It matters very little what our ideal of proportion is, so long as we arrange our normal pattern accordingly, and this we have done in the former pages. A study of these Diagrams will therefore be necessary as we are starting to cut any of the styles which follow, for nearly all the points are formed in the same way with a slight variation in the waist suppression. The first thing to be done is to find out the amount of the disproportion in the particular case we are treating of, and we do this as follows; Subtract four inches from the chest measure in order to get at the ideal waist measure, and then see what difference there is between the ideal waist and the real — thus: 50 chest, minus 4, gives us 46 as the ideal waist; the difference between 46 and 54 is eight inches, and thus a person measuring 50 chest and 54 waist would be dispropor-

tionate to the extent of eight inches. The principle on which the

Variations in cutting

Are made is as follows: First of all the waist suppression at back and side seams is slightly reduced, inasmuch as the hollows of back are less than in the proportionate figure; but the chief variation consists in adding one-third of the disproportion at the sides, leaving the remainder to go on the front. The third added to the sides is applied first of all to reducing the size of the fish — thus in a case of, three inches of disproportion, the amount taken out in the fish under the arms would be reduced to half-an-inch; but when it is more than six inches, then it is necessary to apply an adaptation of the principle explained in Part II. for body coats. This is illustrated in Diagram as follows: From 11¼ to 12½ is one-fourth of the breast, from this square down to 12½ on line 19, and from this point come forward to 12⅞, one-sixth of the disproportion, *minus one inch*, the inch usually taken out of the fish must be considered. Now square line from 12½ to 28½, and 30½ at right angles to 12½ 12⅞, and complete shoulder by it. Measure up the waist in the usual way, and draw a line straight from 28½ through 31½ to J. Now square a line (H) at right angles to 31½ and draw the breast line midway between H and J as illustrated at I. Now fix the hip pocket, finding the position as previously described, but getting it a trifle nearer sideseam than front; X is midway between sideseam and breast line; G, which is centre of flap, is half-an-inch from X, C and B being equal on either side. From C square down to D, and measure from C to line I, and make E the same distance from breast line as C is. Now cut pattern, taking out the V outlined by C D E, closing it at bottom. This will necessitate cutting across pocket mouth and up to the scye, as illustrated by B A, so that it may lie flat on the cloth as shown on small Diagram below hip flap. Any round there is on the front must be well worked up and care must be taken to avoid a bubble forming at C. The closing of D E will necessitate recutting the bottom, taking off from E to F.

THE ALBERT D.B. FROCK OVERCOAT.
Plate 5.

On this Plate we illustrate a garment that bids fair to be the fashionable Overcoat of the immediate future. These Diagrams will therefore be of more than ordinary interest. This style admits of a considerable amount of smartness being infused into it, both as regards finish of edges, seams, &c., as well as also in the style of trimming and position of pockets. In doing so it will be well to keep in mind the tendency there will be of making this like a Livery Overcoat. An outside breast pocket is one of the features; that not only introduces smartness but keeps it quite distinct from any approach to Liveries. The outline of the lapel is another feature that tells in the same direction, so that if these and other points are studied, this can be made a very stylish garment. The materials mostly used are Beavers and Meltons, it being very seldom that cloths of a fancy make are used for this style.

The System

For this, though the same in its general application, has still several important variations, so that we will briefly describe it. The measures taken are the same as for the Chesterfield, plus the length of fashion waist. O to 3 is one-third depth of scye, O 9 is depth of scye, O 17½ is natural waist plus ⅜, and O 20½ is the fashion waist length, usually 2 or 2½ inches below the natural waist. Come in at natural waist from 17½ to ¾, ¾ inch, and draw back seam from O through ¾. Mark off from O to 3 one-twelfth breast and come up ¾ inch. Measure off the width of back plus ¾ inch about 2 inches below point 3 and spring the back scye out slightly as shown, and complete shoulder as illustrated. From ⅜ measure off to 22⅛ the half chest plus 3½ and from this point measure back to 13¾, the across chest measure plus ⅜, and from these points sweep to find the positions of F and D in the usual way. From ⅜ to 9⅞ is one-fourth breast plus ½ inch, point 5 being midway between ⅜ and 9⅞. The width of the back at the waist is made 2½ inches for the 36 and proportionate for the larger sizes, 1¼ inches are taken out from between back and sidebody, and 1 inch between sidebody and forepart, the waist being measured up to 3½ inches over the half waist. To find point A make a pivot of the top of sideseam and sweep from the bottom of sideseam of back and having got this draw a line across from A to B and get the run of the waist seam by measuring up 1 inch and hollowing it accordingly.

The Skirt

Next claims our attention, and in order to produce that we first decide on the degree of fulness desired round the bottom, and if that is desired of moderate fulness we measure down from B 2½ to 3 inches, and draw a line from that point to A as illustrated. From this line come up ¾ inch at ¾ and shape the waist seam of skirt as shown. Now draw a line at right angles from A to 9, and make A G 9 inches always, come out 1 inch from 9, and draw line as shown in Diagram, and beyond that adding on ½ inch of round to allow of its being properly worked up over the hips. On this

line measure off the length, deducting O
20½ from the full length, and applying the
remainder from A to bottom, allowing 1
inch for making up. To get the run of
the front, come out the width of lapel from
B and then come down from A to * the
same as was dropped from B in the first
case, and get the run of front at right angles
to 2½ *. Make the length of front the same
as the length behind, and complete skirt
as per Diagram. If a closer fitting skirt
is desired, reduce the amount from B to
3 and A to * and so in like manner increase
it when a fuller style is wished for.

The Lapel

Is a very important part of this garment,
and one that has a great effect on the style.
Our Diagram illustrates the most usual
style at present. The sewing-to edge is
cut straight, but if it is desired to button
very high up it should be made hollow in
order to get the outer edge of sufficient
length. The width of this lapel is made
2½ at waist, running wider to 3 inches at
the widest part. It is cut about ¾ inch
shorter than the forepart, the fulness being
arranged as per wavy mark at 22⅛ and then
nicely pressed away over the prominence of
breast. The top of lapel is kept well
pointed and moderately rounded on the
outer edge of turn; the Diagram will prove
a good guide in this respect.

The skirt is usually cut wide enough to
allow of a turning in the front, as is usual
with Frock Coats. Tabs are placed in the
pleats as well as in the fronts of skirt; this
keeps the skirt closed at both parts if so
desired. Pockets are sometimes put in the
skirts in the half moon shape; others
have them either on the hips, in the waistseam, or in the pleats.

THE PADDOCK COAT.
Plate 6.

A new style of coat for gentlemen's wear
is not of frequent occurrence, and yet the
great change this coat presents from the
ordinary Chesterfield is so marked, that this
must certainly be looked upon as one of the
most recent "up-to-date" styles. It has
been introduced by those firms who cater
principally for the sporting fraternity, and
is remarkable for the variety of its names,
and yet whether they are called "Paddock",
"Ascot", "Racing", or what else the same
style of coat is referred to in general details.
This may be described as a long Chesterfield with plenty of spring from the waist
downwards. Some define the figure very
closely at the waist, others are made very
loose; some are cut with a sidebody in the
Paletot style, and which we illustrate on
Plate 7, others, as in our Diagram, with a
narrower back, and fish out under the arm
to bring it in to the figure. Some are made
D.B., others S.B., but the larger number
seem to favour the style we have selected,
viz: Fly front with a heavy lapel in D.B.
style. In the matter of pleats there is
a great variety; our Diagram illustrates
the most popular method, viz., an opening
up the back, and side pleats starting from
about 2 inches below the waist. The only
thing which seem to be universal with them
is the length, which reaches to within 8 or
10 inches of the ground.

The Cutting

Of this garment is readily explained by the
Diagram. The sideseam of back is made
fairly round, and the width of back about
4 or 4½ inches wide at the waist; 1¾ inches
is taken out between the back and forepart
at sideseam, and 1 inch is taken out in a

fish under the arm. These quantities are for those intended to define the waist, but as previously stated, many of them are worn very loose, in fact, the appearance is often such as would suggest a ready-made garment of a size too large. The general principles of cut about the shoulders are the same as for a Chesterfield; the shoulder measures being enlarged and the scye deepened in the way we have previously described in these pages. The front is finished by adding not less than 2 inches to make it fly front, and an extra 1½ inches if it is desired to make it double breasted.

The Material

From which these garments are mostly made is Drab Venetian, or Covert Coating as it is often called. It is generally waterproofed before being made up, but the tailor will find it more convenient to have that process done by his wholesale house than attempting to do it himself. Many of the wholesale houses keep it ready waterproofed in stock, so it will be as well to ask if it has been waterproofed when purchasing it. On the page treating of the Covert Coat will be found an excellent receipt for waterproofing, should our readers desire to do this themselves.

This garment being a speciality it will doubtless help our readers if we give a few

The details of Making.

The larger number have the pockets put in crescent shaped, pointing well up in the front; often much more than our Diagram indicates. These are often finished without flaps, the pocket mouths being jeated. The pockets are occasionally made from the same material, and frequently they are patched inside, as a considerable number are made up without any lining, beyond a fairly good facing. There are usually 2 hip pockets,

a breast pocket, and a ticket pocket; the latter being rather larger than usual, say 4 or 4½ inch mouth.

Velvet collars, and cuffs about 2 inches deep, turned up, are often put on this coat, but the more general style is to finish the sleeve with 5 or 6 rows of stitching as our Diagram illustrates; the turn back cuff being objected to on account of its catching the rain when driving through a storm. The edges are mostly finished double stitched, and the seams slated, but as is customary with Covert Coats, this is often varied, the seams being left plain or merely raised with one row of sewing.

We will conclude with a few

General Remarks.

There can be no doubt that this garment will largely take the place of the mackintosh, and consequently should be encouraged by tailors as much as possible, as the sale of mackintoshes can scarcely be looked upon as a likely means of elevating the artistic or scientific phases of tailoring. In making up, any round that is put on the hips of forepart should be well worked forward. When these coats were first introduced, many of them were made with the back on the crease, the opening up the back being at the right hand pleat, but these have mostly given way to the more popular style illustrated on our Diagram sheet.

Some, however, are still made with back on the crease, and this is generally stumped across at the back tack, thus enabling an under back skirt to be placed at the pleats.

THE PALETOT.
Plate 7.

This garment is really a combination of the Chesterfield and Frock Overcoat, presenting a similar appearance to the former in the front, and the latter at the back, and when carefully cut and nicely made, makes a very smart and stylish over-garment. As noticed on our previous page it has recently become decidedly popular though it is by no means a new style, being known in the years that are past as "The Prize Overcoat", "The Paddock, &c.", indeed we believe at one time it formed the subject of a patent. At the present time it is mostly used by sporting gentlemen, though there is every reason to believe it will be-come generally popular in the future, as it makes a very stylish garment and is suit-able for all kinds of material. Our Diagram illustrates the way in which these are now often made in Drab Venetians, the seams raised, the edges swelled, the back cut on the crease, and stumped across the bottom. These, however, are details that are by no means a necessary part of this style of Overcoat, they merely illustrate how it is sometimes finished at the present time.

The Cutting

Is done, as far as the body is concerned, in the same way as the D.B. Frock, with perhaps a trifle under back at waist, but that is always a matter of taste upon which the cutter must use his discretion, so that after all the easiest way of cutting this coat is to take a Frock body, join the forepart and skirt together, and cut the back and sidebody separately as for the frock. The front can be arranged in any style desired, it mattering little whether the fronts are S.B. or D.B., though they are more often made Fly Front, as shown in our Diagram. The plan of drafting the skirt shown on the Diagram is to get point B by sweeping from A by the top of sideseam, and hollow-ing the waistseam of sidebody up 1 inch or to taste. Now come up from B to C 1½ inches. Measure across from B to the level of under arm seam, which is ¼ breast plus ½ inch from centre of back, and from

this point square at right angles to this point and C as illustrated. Come down from C to 9, 9 inches and go out 1, com-pleting the back of skirt by adding on ½ an inch of round.

Practical Details.

In cutting out, there must be provision made for the pleat down the back of skirt in the same way as for a Frock; this should not be less than 1 inch. The amount allowed beyond the breast line is shown as 2 inches, that making good provision for Fly Front. This quantity, however, must be increased at the lapel if the pointed D.B. style is desired; this, however, is not universal. The ordinary turn with the collar and strap placed at about right angles is often used on garments for gentlemen who desire to have nothing obstrusive in their dress. For these too the pockets put straight across at the hips would be the more suitable, though at present the curved pocket mouth with rather large flap are undoubtedly the most in favour. The pockets of this garment may be placed in the pleats if so desired, so that even in the placement of the pockets there is plenty of room for variety. The length generally tends to the long side, certainly reaching to the calf or a little longer, as a short coat of this kind would certainly lose much of its character and become commonplace. The fly would be extended some 7 or 8 inches below the natural waist level, and tabs and buttons neatly secured to the fore-part to close it below, should it be so desired. It is very seldom these coats are ornamented much on the lapel or collar; true they are sometimes finished with velvet collar and turn back cuffs about 2 inches deep, but this is not the general rule, and as for silk facings they are never seen. About 4 buttons would be placed up the front to fasten in the fly, and another at the top to secure right up to the throat in case of stormy weather. A moderately deep collar-fall, about 2½ with tab at front, would complete the neck. A blind fly would be generally arranged down the opening of the back with two or three buttons.

These coats are not often lined with woollen, as they are garments used a good deal for walking, and though worn long are quite a distinct garment from the travelling Ulster, hence Italian cloth would be the more suitable lining, unless the customer will pay the price of silk, though even in this latter case it is doubtful whether it is all advantage in the wear of a long coat of this sort. It certainly would not cling to the legs in walking, but it has the bad habit of wearing out very quickly.

GENTS' ULSTER.
Plate 8.

For travelling purposes, whether it be by road or rail, the Ulster will probably always continue in favour, and so will never get out of fashion, though it may be affected by it in the matter of appendages, such as belt and similar adjuncts. As compared with the Chesterfield the Ulster is very much looser fitting, and often cut to come within a few inches of the ground. As it is intended for travelling purposes its weight and size is not only approved but are amongst its chief characteristics. When cut very loose about the waist it is the custom to put belts at that part, either starting from the sideseams across the back or going round in order to bring them closer to the body, they being invariably finished with 2 buttons to allow of them being made closer if so desired. As a general rule they are cut single breasted, though for certain classes, such as doctors and others who are out during a good deal

at night, they are made D.B. This mode of finish makes the adjustment of the cape more complicated, so that when made with a cape the easiest way is to make it to fasten up to the neck, and finish with a Prussian collar.

The General Features

Of this garment can be best gathered from a study of Diagram 1, which fully explains the cutting. This is done on the same lines as we have previously described for the Chesterfield, with more room infused. The points are marked in inches, and if reproduced by the inch tape will produce a garment suitable for a 36 chest figure with the measure taken over the vest. It will be noticed the amount from back seam to breast line is slightly increased, but this must be done in accordance with the material and lining used. Thus if the material is thick and the lining a heavy woollen plaid, then 4 or even 4½ inches must be added to the half chest measure when marking off the size from 9 to 21¾; and in these cases the fish under the arm need not be taken out, as the garment desired will be a loose fitting one to keep the wearer warm. If made from an ordinary Tweed with Italian cloth lining, then the usual 3½ inches will be sufficient to allow for making up and ease. It will thus be seen there is a good deal of scope for the cutter's judgment in fixing the amount. The opening up the back should start from 9 or 10 inches down from the waist, and in making should be finished with two or three buttons and holes arranged with a blind fly. The spring of the sideseam may be slightly increased, so that it will be better to drop say 1¼ inches instead of 1, at 6 inches in from the sideseam at point 8. The fish under the arm may be omitted if it is to be worn with a belt, but in that case it will be advisable to put that extra size in the garment when measuring up the waist.

The Sleeve, Diagram 2.

This is cut exactly as the Chesterfield, with perhaps a little additional size at elbow and cuff. Ulsters being worn a good deal by gentlemen for driving purposes, the cuffs are often finished with wind cuffs, which is a cuff of flannel or similar material sewn to the lining, and around the bottom of this a piece of elastic is inserted which keeps it close to the wrist. Others have a half-band put across the bottom of cuff with an extra button, so that if desired it can be brought close to the wrist in a similar manner as with wind sleeves, and doubtless these methods add materially to the comforts of a driving Ulster.

Ticket pockets are often put on the sleeve, the left cuff being the position usually selected; the mouth of pocket is generally made to slant up slightly to the hind-arm seam.

The Hood, Diagram 3.

This is a plain business-like affair. There are no fancy plaits, &c., but is cut in such a manner as to provide a covering for the head. The mode of cutting is as follows: Take the back of Ulster, and mark from I to J by the back neck, and continue the curve round to K the half size of neck. Make from I to L not less than 13 or 14 inches; come out at the back seam at M 2 inches, and make from M to N from 12 to 13 inches, and complete the outline of Hood by Diagram. In making this up, I M is sometimes cut on the crease; at others there is a back seam, so as to give it a curve; M to N is sewn up, and a drawing string is put from K to N on both sides; it is generally sewn in with the collar at neck, though it can be made to put on or

off with holes and buttons or hook and loops if preferred.

The Collar, Diagram 4.

This collar has a very deep fall, and may be made to fasten right up to the throat if desired, though it is intended to turn to point A. B is ¼ inch less than the height of stand from the hollow of gorge, and a line is drawn from A B to C; come back from C to D the difference between the stand and fall; D to E is the stand and D to F the fall. F to H and H to G to taste. Make length of collar to the size of neck, and complete as Diagram.

This system is applicable to all kinds of collars intended to roll open, whether high or low, and consequently may be applied to any of the drafts in the book. On Plate 9 we illustrate how to cut a Prussian collar, if that style should be desired for this garment. For Capes to wear with this see Plate 9.

CAPES, HOODS, &c.
Plate 9.

We now take Capes and Hoods, those appendages to the Ulster, which of late years have been so extensively patronized. There are various styles of Capes worn, but by far the larger number are made in the shape illustrated by Diagrams 1, 2, 3 and 4, and known as the half circle Cape. Next in popularity comes the three quarters circle Cape, which is produced by putting the back and front shoulders together in a closing position, and then marking the centre of back by the back seam, and the centre of front by the breast line; marking off the length to taste, making the length of front about 2 inches less than the back, measuring from the bottom of the gorge; whilst the length of the side is about 2½ or 3 inches more than the back, measuring from the middle of the neck. We have not given a Diagram of this style, as it is not so often worn as the styles illustrated on

Diagrams 1 and 2.

In this Diagram the cape is cut with a seam on the top of the shoulder, and the back on the crease; the mode of cutting is to take the back, make point J about 1 inch behind the backseam, and draw a line straight from A to J; mark the neck from A to C, making C 1 inch from B; now mark up from E to W, 1½ inches, and come out from the sideseam at G to H 4 inches, and draw a line from W through H to I, which should be straight after it has passed the prominence of the shoulder. Mark off the length to taste, and shape the bottom as illustrated. To produce the front, take the forepart and reduce the neckpoint at F the same amount as has been added from B to C, then take off at D the same amount as was added from E to W; now draw a line from S to K straight with point M, and come out from L to K 6 inches, and draw line from D through K to N; make the length to harmonize with the back and let the length of front be 2 inches shorter than the back, measuring from the bottom of gorge.

Another Style, Diagrams 3 and 4.

In this method the patterns of back and forepart are placed together, with the shoulder straps touching, and the centre of front running at right angles to the centre of back; when arranged so, advance the front 1 inch and let it drop ½ inch, as illustrated at C H, when the space at C I will be equal to about ⅛ breast (4½ inches for the 36). Draw the backseam by coming out from back of Chesterfield at G 1 inch and mark A B C as the back of Chesterfield. From A to D is ⅓ breast, and D to

E is ⅓ the side of cape is drawn straight from C through E to F. Now arrange the V out of the forepart of the shoulder, as illustrated at C H, and complete the front by the front of the Chesterfield, making the length at L M N as before described for Diagrams 1 and 2. Take out from 3 to 4 inches at E K more or less, as the cape is desired close or tight fitting, and draw line from C K L straight. If any round is put on here it will appear full at the seam. The V taken out at H gives a different style to this cape, and by this means the seam is kept well back, so that it can scarcely be seen in front; the extra length of shoulder at C end of V is fulled on in the form of a sleeve head, which gives a good style to this cape. There are many

Different Modes of Front.

The solid line illustrates the front, which would be suitable for a garment fastening up to the neck with a Prussian collar, the cape being buttoned through also; the dot and dash line from I to J and N shows how the front of cape should be cut away if it is desired to have a collar and turn to the Ulster, the part lowered at J being made to follow the crease row. The dotted lines at O P illustrate the mode of cutting double breasted capes, the lapel being made from 3 to 3½ inches beyond the breast line. These double breasted capes are generally made to be worn as separate garments, and are faced and lined in the ordinary way for a coat, pockets being arranged in the bottom corner of front. These styles are either finished with hooks and loops at the neck, or have a narrow band put on with holes to fasten over buttons put on the stand of the collar of the coat; they are generally made detachable, it being very unusual with them to be finished, sewn in with the collar at gorge, though this method may be adopted if desired.

The Hood. — Diagram 5.

This is another style of hood to what we illustrated on the Diagram Plate showing Ulsters, &c. It is cut by placing the shoulder point of back and forepart together as at A, and the distance from D to F about ⅛ breast. From W to B is about 14 or 15 inches, and from B to C is about 1 inch less, *i.e.*, 13 or 14 inches; the width at V is 1 or 1½ inches; V F is the same as the front gorge, and F A D is a V taken out, W B is cut on the crease, and the bottom edge at DC is sewn together, as are the sides of V at F D A.

The Collar. — Diagram 6.

This Diagram illustrates how to cut the Prussian collar, line O 8½ is straight, and is half the size of gorge, 8½ to 1 is 1 inch, and the sewing to edge of collar is shaped hollow as from 1 to O; make the depth of stand from O to 1½ to taste or customer's wish, and continue across to front, where it seldom exceeds ½ inch, from 1½ to 4½ is the depth of fall, in this case 3 inches; a little spring is given to the back seam, and the shape of front is finished to taste. A very little stretching of the fall edge will be sufficient, the principal amount of stretching being required at the sewing to edge where it is hollow.

This is the style of collar generally used for garments buttoning up to the throat.

THE SCARBORO'
SLEEVELESS ULSTER AND CAPE.
Plate 10.

The Scarboro' Sleeveless Ulster and Cape is one of the most popular Overgarments at the present time, and is especially suitable for travelling purposes, for which it possesses many features to recommend it. It is roomy and comfortable, easily put on, and is free from the discomfort frequently experienced in the Inverness when the arms are raised or brought forward; and, as compared to the Ulster, it has far greater freedom and permits of its being worn over any kind of undercoat without disarranging it. This makes it an ideal travelling garment, especially when made of thick Cheviot or Frieze, and the cape cut long enough to well cover the hand.

This style of garment is admirably suited for waterproofs, the very deep scye-and easy fit affords such an excellent opportunity for ventilation that all difficulty to the removal of this greatest objection to waterproofs is done away with. A reference to

Diagram on Plate 10

Will show the special features of the body-part of this garment. The back is cut on the crease, the shoulder is made slightly narrow, the scye is lowered to within 2 inches, more or less, of the waist, and the general style of cut is on the principle of the Sac Overcoat. Thus, there is no suppression of the waist at sideseam, but the extra spring for the hips, &c., is gôt below that point (7½) in the same way as for a Chesterfield, coming in from point 7½ to 13½ 6 inches, and dropping 1 or 1¼ if extra spring is desired. When the body of these garments is made long — and they frequently measure 52 or 54 in length — it is customary to arrange an opening with a blind fly at each sideseam, otherwise it would be difficult to walk in it.

They are generally made single breasted, button through, but occasionally this is varied by the double breast, these, however, are the exception. The pockets are mostly patched in a similar manner to an Inverness, to which garment it bears so striking a resemblance that some call it an Inverness, with the cape going all round. The neck is generally finished with a Prussian collar, the exception being when the cape is arranged as a separate garment and not sewn to the neck at the collar seam as usual, then the body part is generally finished with a stand collar, and the cape either finished with heavy collar and turn, or — without collar — made to fasten round the neck with hooks and eyes.

The Cape

Usual for this class of garment we have illustrated on Plate 9, the style being known as the Half Circle Cape. They are usually cut to cover the sleeves of the undercoat, and of sufficient fulness to allow free use of the arms; but it will be well here to remark that heavy material looks fuller than thin goods, so it will be well to cut them slightly closer fitting when made from heavy Friezes and Meltons. Some means should be provided of securing the cape to the body part at both back and front so as to prevent it blowing over the head in boisterous weather. The best way of doing this is to put a tab on the centre of the back of the cape, and one at each front, buttons being placed to the body part at corresponding positions. It is a very good plan to arrange a pocket in the bottom part of the cape facing, as it enables the wearer to keep the cape in position and keep his hands warm at the same time, both features of importance in a garment intended to defy the stormy blast and the winter's cold. There a kind of backed material used for this garment sometimes that has the lining and outside all in one substance — that is, there would be a Cheviot or Frieze outside, with a bright woollen plaid inside, and as many experience a little difficulty in making up this we will explain the best method of doing so. The fronts are made up with facings in the usual way, with canvas, &c., through

the forepart, stays are put at the corner of the pockets and covered with circular pieces of the material felled over them. The seams are best raised and double stitched — thus on the sideseam of the forepart an inlay would be left, and the back cut nett, the back would then be seamed to the forepart, turned over, and double stitched, and then the inlay of forepart cut off up to the second row of stitching, and then, if fraying is to be feared, the edges of the forepart felled on to the back. With the scye, the edge may either be turned in and double stitched to harmonize, or it may be bound with Galoon or Prussian binding, that making a thin and neat scye. Each season brings garments of this class more and more into note and wear, and we doubt not but they will be in good demand for many years to come; for when comfort and utility is combined in a gent's garment it does not soon go out of fashion.

THE COACHING OVERCOAT OR D.B. SAC. Plate 11.

Our next Plate illustrates the very loose style of Overcoat known as the Coaching Sac. This garment has many distinctive features, and it is one that produces a very smart appearance on the box. It is one of the heaviest types of Overcoats worn by gentlemen, and being invariably lined with Tweed and made from heavy Beaver or Melton, it would prove a very cumbersome garment for ordinary wear. Anyone, however, who has had a little experience in driving knows that it requires a warm thick coat to enable one to face the biting weather frequently experienced on the box, and this is the garment that those who patronize coaching seem to favour most.

The material from which it is made is a Drab Beaver or Melton; the edges are left raw, the facings lapped on to the Tweed lining and jimped out. The seams of this coat are slated and double stitched; the pockets, of which there are generally a goodly number, are large and usually covered with good size flaps, as it would not do to provide receptacles for the rain to fill, such as welt pockets would be.

The Buttons

On these coats are one of its most conspicuous features, and are invariably large in size — say as big as a five shilling piece. Buffalo horn, four holes, are sometimes used, but more generally it is a white pearl with a fancy design, such as a coach or a monogram, is engraved on these to order. Any of the wholesale trimming houses get this done, and the cost is not great. Two rows of buttons of this size and style look very bold, but it is quite in keeping with coaching dress generally, and there can be no doubt it looks effective. The distance the buttons are apart, of course, varies, but they should not be less than 4 inches, or buttons so large as these will look crowded. This necessitates a good overlap being left in the front, certainly not less than 3½ inches beyond breast line, and in the larger sizes 4 inches will not be any too much.

The Cutting.

Whilst the general instructions given at the beginning of this Work forms the basis on which this, as well as all other Overcoats shown in this Work are cut, there are variations in some of them of a somewhat important character. This in an example. Instead of suppressing the back at 17½ we actually add on 1 inch and draw the centre of back straight from O to point 1 to the bottom; and instead of suppressing the sideseam 1 inch, we let the forepart overlap the back 1 inch, drawing the sideseam straight in each case, the principle involved

the same amount as is added beyond the construction line at waist. Of course, it will be understood that point 21½ on the waist line is not found by measuring up as for the normal figure, but by squaring down from point 21½ of the depth of scye line; but if the waist is very large then measure across from 17½ the half waist measure, and 5½ inches. Some may think 3½ inches is barely enough to allow over the half breast measure, but our experience goes to show that it will prove enough even for thick Melton with woollen lining, as the style of cutting beyond the construction line of back and of overlapping the forepart and back gives an increase in the size. If these are desired very loose fitting it will be quite permissible to deepen the scye more; indeed a very safe guide in this respect is to deepen the scye the same amount as allowed beyond construction line at 17½ and from 8 to 9.

The Collar.

This is generally cut very wide and heavy, the inside collar being stitched in slanting rows of machine sewing, and when the outside is covered with velvet, as it often is, it is the custom to strap the edge with the same material as the coat, the width of this being so arranged as to allow the stitching to go round this the same width as the edges of the coat. In giving this garment out to the workman it will be well to caution him against using a stitch too small on the machine; or, in making, the weight of the parts will tear the seam open, result not to be desired in material so expensive as that from which these coats are made.

THE NEW STYLE OF INVERNESS.
Plate 12.

For some seasons past the Inverness has held an important position in the list of Overgarments for gentlemen's wear. The easy freedom with which they can be put on or off has recommended them, especially for wear over dress clothes, whilst the comfort and warmth make them specially suitable for travelling purposes, so that we find them one of the most popular garments for all classes. The clergyman wears it made from black Vicuna, and the sporting gent patronizes the same style of garment but made from some horsey pattern of tweed; the scope offered in the selection of material is quite wide enough to suit all classes.

The Leading Features

Of the new style of Inverness we will describe as made in West End firms at the present time. The old style of Inverness was remarkable for its size, as will be gathered from Plate 13. But now they are generally cut very much closer fitting, and although there is still plenty of ease in them, yet the size and shape of the body are taken into consideration a little in drafting the pattern. The back is cut very much closer fitting than the old style, but that necessitates an ample allowance of spring on the wing, otherwise a tightness would be experienced when moving the arms. Room for the shoulders is provided by the sleeve head arrangement of the wing, which we shall describe more fully in dealing with

The System.

Draw line O 50, O 3, and mark off from O to 9 the depth of scye; O 3¼, ½ inch more than one-third O 9; O to 7½ is the natural waist, plus ½ inch, and continue on to 50 full length desired, plus seams.

Draw lines at right angles to point O 3¼, 9, 7½, and mark off from O to 3, ⅙ breast; from 3¼ to 7¾, the across back measure, plus 1 inch; from 9 to 21½ the chest measure, plus 3½ inches. From 7½ come back to ¾, ¾ to 1 inch, and draw centre of back from O through ¾. Square down from point 7¾ for the sideseam of back, draw shoulder seam and neck by the points previously obtained, coming up ¾ from point 3, and the back is complete, so we now turn our attention to

The Forepart.

From 21½ come back to point 13⅛ the across chest measure, plus ⅜, and find the neck point F by sweeping from 13⅛ by the front shoulder measure, plus ⅜, and adding the usual 1 inch to 21½ when making the second sweep. Point D is found by adding ⅜ to the over shoulder measure, deducting the quantity from 9 to W and by the remainder sweeping from point 13⅛ to find D, but the width of the forepart shoulder is generally about 1½ or 2 inches, the scye being cut away to about 2 inches above the natural waist line as at point 1, the sideseam of forepart is allowed to overlap in accordance with the amount of ease desired, in the present instance this is 1 inch at waist, and a line is drawn from 7¾ through 1 to the bottom, From F to V and V to I are each ⅙ of the breast, and the breast line is then got from V to 21½ below which the centre line is drawn at right angles to line 9 21½. Add ¾ inch to the length of forepart in front, so as to get a continuous run with the back. Add on about 1½ inches of button stand and the forepart is complete, so we turn our attention to

The Wing,

Which is the special feature of the Inverness. The gorge from F to I is the same as the forepart; 1 inch is added on at front at natural waist line so as to counteract any tendency there may be to open. The shoulder is continued from F to D, and made a full ¼ of an inch narrower than the back, and draw a line from D in the direction of 13⅛ as would be usual in shaping the scye, this is followed for about 3 or 4 inches from the shoulder seam. Now draw a line from 7¾ through point 9, and connect 7¾ with the forepart as illustrated. The length of the wing is purely a matter of taste, and is usually arranged by putting the sleeve to the hindarm pitch just below 7¾, and swinging it round to get the length of the back part of the wing continuing across the forepart straight. As will be seen, this wing is intended to button through the front, and must be finished at the neck either with a stand or Prussian collar. If desired to be finished with a collar and turn, it will be necessary either to finish the forepart as a no-collar vest, and arrange the collar on the wing, or else to cut the wing away about 2 inches behind the breast line and fasten it to the forepart with tabs. It may be of importance to some that we add a few

Hints on Making.

The back is generally cut on the crease, the pockets being usually patched and finished with holes and buttons. The style of finish at the neck most popular is the Prussian collar. Pockets are often put in the wing, which enables the cape to be kept down in boisterous weather. The body is lined either with Italian or Woollen Plaid, and the wing is invariably lined with a satin lining. In putting the fulness in the sleeve head of the wing, arrange it as for an ordinary sleeve head, and if necessary carry the V a little lower. A good plan to get the correct amount of fullness is to draw a line from the hind arm pitch of sleeve parallel to 9 23, and where that crosses the

wing put it to the same point of back. In sewing the sideseam be careful to preserve the correct balance at 1, and it will be found necessary to well stay it at that part. The wing is left loose about 3 or 4 inches from the bottom, a tack being placed at that part. This we think embraces the special features of the Inverness as it is now being made.

Inverness with Sleeves.

Occasionally customers order sleeves to be added to their Inverness, and this, of course, necessitates the scye being cut as close as for an ordinary Chesterfield. The shoulder is made the same width as the Chester, and the whole of the scye from shoulder point of back to shoulder point of front is cut on the forepart, the rule being to continue the sideseam of forepart up to point 7¾ as per dotted line, and shaping the scye just the same as for a Chester, and arranging the sleeve as usual. This does not interfere with the run of sideseam, or the method of sewing the waist, forepart, and back together, as the scye is quite independent of the sideseam.

THE OLD STYLE OF INVERNESS.
Plate 13.

With the view of making the present Work a comprehensive one on the subject of Overcoat cutting, we give the old style of Inverness a place in its pages; not so much on account of any anticipated revival of this style as a fashionable garment, but rather because there is a likelihood of a continued demand for it; for whilst the new styles has many characteristic features which commend it for smartness and style, there is still a lack of that free and easy character which has always been a marked feature in the Inverness.

The old style of Inverness may be described as a cape cut more or less full, with a forepart added. The easiest way of producing them is by the aid of a block pattern of a Chesterfield, and this is the plan we now adopt; but should any of our readers prefer to work it out according to system, we have clearly defined all the points on the Diagram, so that they may use the more scientific way if they choose. But we prefer to be practical, and as we cater for practical men we will describe what appears to us to be the most

Practical Method of Cutting an Inverness.

Ease and simplicity, accuracy and speed, are all combined in this method. First select a Chesterfield block of the size of your customer, or if he is a very unusual shape, draft one out to the measure taken on him direct, on the lines laid down in former pages. Place the back in the position shown, come out from waist 1 inch and draw the centre seam of the back straight through this from neck point to the bottom; follow the neck and shoulder of Chesterfield back, but from point W opening out, letting it come through a point 3 inches from the back on the depth of scye line, below which it should be continued at the same angle; but there must not be any round to it, otherwise the seam will appear bobbly. It is not advisable to cut the back much fuller than this, as it makes the cape more difficult to fit; but if a small cape is desired then the back must be wider than when a full cape is intended to be added. The harmony of the various parts of the same garment is always important in cutting, and especially so in this garment.

The Forepart.

Take the Chesterfield forepart, mark round the front edge (this is presuming the Chesterfield has been cut the same style as the Inverness is intended to be in the front of the gorge and the shoulder for about 1½ inches from F, and from this point form the scye in the style shown in the Diagram, carrying it down to within about 1½ or 2 inches of the waist, and draw the sideseam of forepart straight to the bottom of sideseam of Chesterfield, as sufficient extra spring has been allowed in the back without any extra being given to the front. Now, although we have laid down positive quantities, in many instances, such as for the scye, there is considerable scope allowed in this garment. The shoulder may be made wider or narrower, the scye may be carried lower or brought closer up. We have merely indicated the general style, considering this to be the best basis for the inexperienced cutter to start from. We will now pass on to deal with

The Wing.

Take the forepart of the Chester and mark round the gorge and across the shoulder to D, and from this point the degree of the fulness is varied. For a close fitting cape come beyond the sideseam of Chesterfield ⅙ of the breast, but if an easier style is desired come out ¼ or even ⅓ breast, and from this point to D shape the side part of the wing. The length of the wing is got by first marking the balance mark to correspond with the pitch of the sleeve on the wing, as illustrated by ÷ mark about 2 inches below D, and from this sweep by the length of the hindarm of the sleeve till it begins to curve upward to the front; where this begins it should continue across to the front straight, this will be readily gathered from the Diagram.

At the bottom of cape it should extend 1½ or 2 inches beyond the front of Chesterfield, so as to prevent any tendency there may be to fly open at that part in wear.

The remarks we have made on the details of style and finish on the more modern style apply with equal force to this garment, so that it is quite unnecessary for us to again repeat them, the more especially as we have infused as many details as possible in the Diagram.

FUR LINED OVERCOAT.
Plate 14.

If there is one style of Overcoat that is less affected by fashion than another it is the Fur Lined Overcoat. This is doubtless largely due to the fact that they are worn more by elderly gentlemen, who care more for comfort than style. It is true more of them are to be seen some seasons than others, whilst we also find that some particular kind of fur is more used than another, but this does not affect the general character of this garment, which may be described as a loose fitting Chesterfield with roll collar and good overlap. The foreparts are frequently ornamented with tabular braid, finished at the end in the form of either crow's toes, as shown on Diagram, or with drop loops in the style of an Infantry Patrol Jacket. These are made to extend beyond the front from ½ to ¾ inch, so as to allow of the loop going easily over the olivettes placed on the opposite side. As a general rule only one side is braided. Many gentlemen, however, prefer a quieter and neater style, and so dispense with the braiding altogether; in this case loops of cord are placed on the edge to fasten over the buttons on the forepart, button holes being considered impracticable through the fur.

The Cutting

Is fully illustrated on the Diagram, but in order to emphazise the various points we will direct attention to them. The back is only hollowed a ¼ inch, and the sideseam suppressed barely ¾, the fish being omitted in this case, as it would be out of harmony with the general easy character of the coat to get it close fitting at the waist. Fully 1 inch extra must be allowed at breast for making up, but the omission of the fish under the arm provides ½ an inch, so that for ordinary fur 4 inches over the half chest will be enough, though a little more than this will not be detrimental, as ease is an important feature. In dealing with the shoulder measures it will be well to increase them fully ½ an inch instead of ⅜, as the fur being thicker than the woollen plaid generally used for lining it is necessary to give a little extra length to the shoulder. Add ½ an inch to the across chest measure as well as the natural waist length, and in cutting the sleeves see they are cut wide enough, as fur takes up a lot of room. For a normal figure or any who are fairly proportionate, square down from 22 for the run of front, but if the figure is inclined to be stout allow rather more — say ½ inch, beyond what is allowed over the half breast. The amount of overlap should be fully 3 inches, but, of course, this can be varied as for ordinary style. The Diagram illustrates how the gorge is cut when a roll collar is desired. The system for collar cutting previously given answers well for a roll collar, though it will be understood that the collar in this case comes to the end of the gorge.

Fur Linings

Are obtained from various wholesale furriers, who will supply them all made up ready to be inserted, the usual plan being to send them on the pattern of the coat with instructions as to the kind of fur desired. The fur on the collar and cuffs is not always the same as the body lining, though it is sometimes so, more generally, however, it is better and more costly. The edges have an edging of the fur sewn in to give the impression that the body lining is the same as the collar, &c. Fur as a general rule is made with the pile to run up, not down like cloth. It is generally interlined with wadding, which gives it a much richer effect. It is sewn together edge and edge with a kind of serging stitch, or what the dressmakers would call over-sewing. When it is found necessary to cut it never use scissors, as they would not only cut the skin but also the fur, the proper way is to lay the flesh side uppermost and cut it with a sharp knife or razor. By this method the skin only is cut, and when this is joined together the fur goes over the join and hides it. There is another points to be borne in mind in making these garment. All pressing that is necessary must be done before the fur is put in, as steam contracts the skin and makes it go hard and lumpy, so that it must not be allowed to come near it or the fur may be spoilt. Fur being expensive it naturally follows that garments of this class are very costly, ranging from 6 to 100 guineas, according to the mode of finish and the kind of fur and material used. Individual fancy as in every other kind of garment decides many details, such as shade and kind of material; the most popular, however, is either Blue or Plum colour Beaver, and the fur either Astrachan or Sealskin.

The length is usually about 44 inches for a 5 feet 9 figure, and sometimes the back is cut on the crease.

MILITARY OVERCOATS.
Plates 15 and 16.

To the most superficial student of Military garments it must be apparent that civilian attire has been and still is largely affected by the regulation garments worn by the officers of the army, and the more careful observer will feel himself bound to admit that those responsible for the existing regulations have been men of practical ability, who have experimented with various ideas, till the useful and the ornamental have been combined. It is true there is not much of an ornamental nature about the Military Overcoat of today; they are distinguished more for their utility, for these garments enable the wearer to face the snowstorm with comparative impunity. As is pretty well known the War Office publish when necessary a book containing the dress regulations of the Army — a book remarkable for its conciseness and scope. The extracts which we give below are taken from that work. In addition to this sealed patterns of all the regulation garments are kept at the War Office for the inspection of those tailors who have to cater for Military officers, so that every possible facility exists for the obtaining information on these subjects. There are

Various Styles of Military Overcoats

Each specially adapted to the wants of the intended wearer; and as we have carefully examined the details of each of the sealed patterns at the War Office the accompanying Diagrams will be found especially useful to those who live at a distance, as well as supplying much worthy the careful study of the cutter who never has to cater for Military customers.

The War Office patterns consists of four distinct types — two double breasted and two single breasted. The former for Staff or General Officers, Infantry, Rifles and Engineers, and the latter for Cavalry and Artillery. The Diagrams are reduced models of the War Office patterns, the quantities marked on them being the actual dimensions of these. The dotted lines represent the normal Chesterfield pattern, so that a good idea can readily be obtained of the variation necessary when cutting the Military Over-coat.

The Official Regulations

For these garments run as follows, taking first the general instructions:

Great-Coats and Capes.

Great-coats will be made according to the following description: —

Milled cloth, double breasted, to reach within a foot of the ground. Stand and fall collar, 4½ inches deep with a fly to cover the band of the cape when buttoned on. Loose round cuffs, 6 inches deep; 2 pockets with flaps at the waist in front, 2 openings behind, at the sideseams, with pointed flaps 11 inches long; a pocket inside the left breast. A slit in the lest side for hilt of sword to pass through. An opening behind, 19 inches long, with a fly; 2 rows of buttons down the front, 6 in each row, the top buttons 6 inches apart, the bottom ones 4 inches; 3 buttons on each skirt flap, the centre one to close the pocket; 4 small buttons at the opening behind; and 5 flat buttons under the fly at the collar. A cloth back-strap, attached to the top of the skirt-flap, to confine the coat at the waist; 2 hooks and eyes to the collar. Shoulder straps on the coat, of the same material as the garment; a small button of the pattern authorized for the respective services at the top. Badges of rank in gold; in bronze for Rifle Regiments. Cape of the same cloth as the coat, and long enough to cover the knuckles; 4 small buttons in front; to fasten at the neck with a leather strap, runner and buckle. Four cloth tabs with button holes in the lining at the bottom, one on either side in front and two in the rear, so as to secure the cape to the bottom buttons of the coat in front and to the top buttons on the flaps behind.

In the case of the Mounted Officers for whom the above pattern of coatis authorized, the following modifications will be made: — The opening of the coat behind will be long enough to reach to the cantle of the saddle, and a gusset will be introduced commencing at the top of the slit and extending downwards to about 24 inches, with about 19 inches' width at the bottom. A tab with button hole at the bottom of the gusset to close it when the coat is worn on foot. A small pocket with a flap at the back of the left sleeve. On the inside of each skirt a cloth band with button to secure the skirts over the knees when the coat is worn on mounted duties. The four buttons at the opening behind are omitted. The coat to reach to the ankles when worn on foot.

STAFF OFFICERS OVERCOATS.
Plate 15.

The official regulations are as follows: —

Great-Coats and Capes.

Blue milled cloth, of the pattern described above, lined with scarlet rattinett; the collar lined with blue velvet. Shoulder straps of the same material as the garment; a small gilt button at the top. Badges of rank in gold.

Our own observations are embodied as far as possible in the Diagram. The position, size and shape of pockets, belt, straps, &c., &c., are all clearly defined. The cuffs, the pockets in the undersleeve are illustrated better than any written explanation could do. The cape is a ¾ circle, finished at the neck with stand collar with 5 holes. The collar on the coat is arranged as Diagram 5, the shaded parts coming down over the buttons on the collar stand, so that when the collar is turned down there is the appearance of the cape being sewn in with the neck seam, whereas really it is detachable. The tab illustrated on the cape is intended to be worn fastened to one of the buttons on the forepart. The dotted angular strap at the bottom of forepart is a plain piece of Melton, properly stayed, to allow of the Overcoat being fastened round the legs when worn on horesback. The gusset is illustrated up the back, and this is a special provision for wear when riding; the tab shown at bottom fastening it together when on foot. The rattinett referred to for lining has much the appearance of shaloon.

Diagrams 7, 8 and 9.
Engineers, Infantry and Rifles Overcoats.

For Engineers the official regulations run as follows: —

Great-Coat and Cape.

Blue cloth, of the pattern previously described, lined with scarlet shaloon, the collar lined with Garter Blue Velvet. Shoulder straps of the same material as the garment; a small button of regimental pattern at top. Badges of rank in gold.

Further details in making are edges swelled, large inside breast pocket with welt. Pocket in sideseam extending 7 inches below bottom of pointed flap in sideseam, as well as jeated pockets in front.

The Infantry and Rifles have the same pattern coat with different buttons. The official regulations are as follows: —

Great-Coat.

Grey cloth of regimental pattern. Shoulder straps of the same material as the garment; a small button of regimental pattern at top. Badges of rank in gold.

Our own observations in addition to these showed there was no pocket either in the sideseams or inside the breast, but the sideseam was open at the pointed flaps, so that the hand could go into the trouser pockets if so desired. The remaining details are all embodied on the Diagram.

CAVALRY AND ARTILLERY CLOAKS.
Plate 16.

The Cavalry Cloak, shown on Diagrams 1, 2, 3, bears a very strong resemblance to that of the Staff Officer with the exception that it is single breasted, and the cape has a V out of the neck, so making it a little closer fitting. We find the only difference between a Cavalry Cloak and that worn by the Dragoons, Dragoon Guards and the Lancers, they being sections of the Cavalry, lies in the colour of the lining and the pattern of the buttons, each section having special regimental designs. The following are the official regulations: —

Cloak and Cape.

Blue cloth of the same pattern as for rank and file, to reach to the ankles when worn on foot. White shaloon lining in the 6th Dragoon Guards, of scarlet in other regiments. Collar of cape of white cloth in the 6th Dragoon Guards, of blue cloth in other regiments. Gilt buttons of regimental patterns. Shoulder straps of the same material as the garment, a small button at top. Badge of rank in gold. The pockets are large and placed slanting up in front, the one in the undersleeve being also fairly roomy. This Overcoat is very plain and business-like, and we do not think anyone need have any trouble in making one from these instructions and Diagrams.

The last illustration we give is of the

This has many special features, particularly in connection with the sleeve, notably no hindarm to the sleeve, and the wedge shaped gusset cut on the forepart at scye to allow of ease being infused to the sleeve head. There are no flap pockets either in the sleeve or forepart, the pockets being put in the sideseam without a flap of any kind. The dotted band 17 on the forepart shows the way the waist belt is fastened up when not used to make the waist fit close: —

The official regulations are as follows: —

Cloak.

Blue cloth with sleeves. Stand-and-fall collar, with 3 black hooks and eyes in front (see Diagram 7) and 3 small flat silk buttons at the bottom to fasten to the cape. Round loose cuffs 6 inches deep. A pocket in each sideseam outside, and one in the left breast inside; four buttons down the front. A cloth back strap to fasten with a large flat silk button at the top of each pocket; a similar button in front on the right to hold the end of the back strap when it is not buttoned across behind. White shaloon lining; the cloak to reach within eight inches of the ground. Shoulder straps of the same material as the garment; a small button of regimental pattern at the top. Badges of rank in gilt metal.

Cape.

Blue cloth 32 inches deep, lined with white shaloon; a cloth band round the top to fasten with a cloth strap and black buckle, and a fly inside the band with 3 button holes for attaching cape to cloak; 3 buttons down front. The lining of the cape shown is terminated 2¾ inches from the bottom edge, the fly on the inside of the cape collar was made up of silesia; there was a narrow facing up the front of the cape. The inside breast pocket had a 9 inch welt, with a depth of 15 inches, the back end was 5½ inches below the scye and the most forward point 7½ inches from the front edge. The various quantities are all clearly marked on these Diagrams, so that the only other thing that remains for us to point out that in a study of these specialities the average cutter who has only to cater for civilian attire will find many points of interest as well as many novel ideas and new combinations which will open up large possibilities if he has any skill as a designer.

One other point, viz., these Overgarments are for officers, they being the only class who come to the tailor for their garments, the rank and file having their wants supplied from the Pimlico factory, where the Government undertake the making of all the garments worn by Tommy Atkins and Co.

NAVAL GREAT-COAT.
Plate 17.

Much that we have stated in connection with Military Overcoats will apply equally to those for Naval Officers. The regulation pattern is clearly defined, and a sealed specimen garment, correct in detail, is deposited at the Admiralty Office, Whitehall, for the inspection of those who desire to make themselves acquainted with the particulars of the various details. As will be gathered from the Diagram, it is a distinct type of garment to any other we have illustrated in this Volume, the especial feature which makes it such is the large box pleat down the centre of back which is secured at the top by the triangular tack at the top, and kept close to the figure at waist by the aid of the belt.

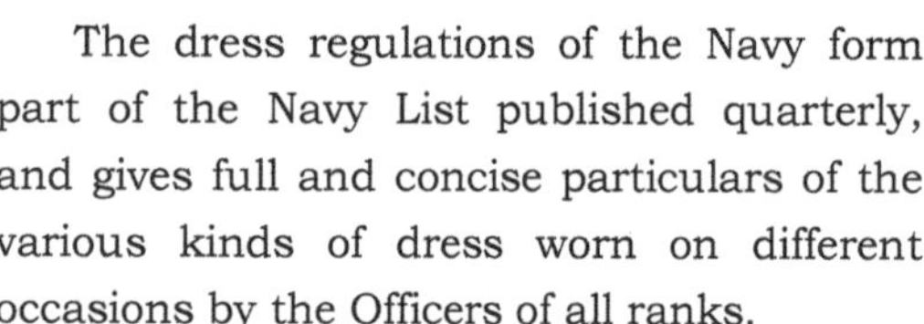

The dress regulations of the Navy form part of the Navy List published quarterly, and gives full and concise particulars of the various kinds of dress worn on different occasions by the Officers of all ranks.

The Official Regulations

For the Naval Great-Coat are as follows: —

For all Officers.

To be worn over full dress and other uniform. Blue cloth. Length to come to 14 inches from the ground. Double breasted. Six buttons on each side. The bottom button not to come below the level of hips. A plait down the back with an opening 18 inches long, with a fly and 4 plain small buttons. A cloth strap behind with a button hole at each end, 8 inches apart, and 2 corresponding uniform buttons to confine the waist to required size. Stand and fall collar, with hook and eye in collar seam. Edge of coat to be double stitched; the shoulders fitted with straps if required. When the sword is worn with this coat it has the hilt arranged to come outside the slit at the side, which necessitates it being hooked up. The provision for this is seen in the vertical flap on the waist line, this is only placed on the left side.

This coat is lined down to the level of hip pocket, the lining being stitched through in the manner indicated by Diagram. The details of this garment are clearly brought out in the Diagram, and from it will be seen there are two tabs with corresponding buttons below the sixth button on front, but this would not show.

The Cutting

Of this coat is very similar to other Over-coats in the shoulder section. The back is not hollowed at all, and the plait down the centre is provided for by allowing 8 inches a side beyond the centre. The back is cut rather wide at the waist, to allow of the correct distance appearing between the buttons; the sideseam has a little suppression, say ½ inch, and the spring over the hips is arranged in the usual way. The amount of overlap in the front beyond the breast line is 3½ inches all down the front, and this necessitates the buttons in front being a good distance apart. The style of collar is what is known in the trade as a Prussian collar, and we give a Diagram of this of the correct dimensions as regards stand and fall. O 1 is the sewing-to edge; this being cut hollow provides sufficient length of fall edge for a garment fastening up to the throat. The sleeves are cut full and easy, but have no specially distinguishing features, a row of stitching being placed to form the cuff. This is the regulation Great Cloak of the Navy; there are, however,

Other Varieties,

Notably a Mackintosh Coat and Cape, which has the cape made detachable. The colour of this is dark blue, and the material from which it is made is optional, though it must be made of the same style as the Admiralty pattern. These can be obtained from any wholesale firm of mackintosh manufacturers, so that we need not dwell further on these, as it would not pay tailors to make them, even if they cared to do so. In addition to this there is a Boat Cloak. The shape of this is very similar to the Scarboro, there being no sleeves but a fairly full cape. The cloth is blue and the lining of the cape is white, and that of the coat black. This garment is not enforced, but if the officer chooses to wear one of this kind, its use is restricted to boat service or other than drills, exercise and evening wear; thus it will be seen it forms a kind of undress Overcoat.

Formerly the Naval Overcoat was a kind

of D.B. Frock, but this is now obsolete, the styles we have enumerated being the only ones now officially recognized.

LIVERY OVERCOATS.
Plate 18.

The Livery Overcoat of the present date is pretty well confined to the style illustrated on this Plate. The old style of Caped Box Coat has given way to the Mackintosh, and so the field is left clear for this style, to have undisputed sway. As will be gathered from the Diagram, the Livery Overcoat is a double breasted Frock with lapels sewn on, fastening right up to the throat. There is the regulation number of 6 buttons up the fronts, the bottom one coming in the waist seam, and the top one so arranged that the end of the collar can be slipped under it in the style shown on the figure and Diagram. The skirt is cut full and long, the length varying for the different classes of servants; as example, the Groom's Overcoat only reaches to just over the knee, the Coachman's comes to the middle of the top part of the top boots, whilst the Footman's comes to within 6 or 7 inches of the ground. If any variation is made in the degree of fullness it should be to give the coachman rather more than ordinary.

Practical Details.

The sleeves are cut fairly full, and are finished with 5 rows of sewing round the bottom; they are lined with linen so as to slip on as easily as possible. The body of the coat is lined with Tweed, and the skirts with shaloon. It will be observed that we have represented on the Diagram, the seams slated and double stitched, this arrangement is very popular with many families, but it must not be regarded as a universal regulation, for there are quite as many made with plain seams. It is, however, the universal custom to double stitch the edges; the collar, lapel, flaps (if any), and side edge down the front of skirt and the back tack with the edge turned in. The side edge put on these coats is 12 inches long for all servants, the outline of this being clearly defined on the Diagram. It is purely for ornament, and simply consists of a piece of cloth stitched on to the back skirts in the style shown, with 3 buttons plugged on it, one on the hips, one at the bottom, and one slightly nearer the top than the bottom one. All buttons used for ornament only must be plugged, or in other words, the shank of the button forced through the cloth and a plug of linen passed through the eye and firmly secured above and below, this preventing the falling off appearance seen when they are sewn on: Those done in this way (plugged) are those placed on the left breast and the side edges.

The Pockets

Placed in these garments vary for different servants. The Footman has two pleat pockets, an inside breast pocket, and a ticket pocket in the waist seam. For Coachmen and Grooms there are pockets placed on the hips at waist seam with flaps over them, the size of flap for the 36 breast being about 10½ by 3½ inches. The ticket pocket is frequently put in the forepart with a curved mouth and flap over it; at other times the flaps and pocket mouth are both square, whilst occasionally the ticket pocket is put in the waist seam; the breast pocket is put inside, as for the footman. The pockets in all these coats should be made from strong material. Trouser pocketing answers well, as these garments last a long time and the pockets have to stand a fair amount of wear.

The material mostly used for these garments is Drab Devon, but Drab is by no means the only shade. Blues, Browns and Greens are represented in every possible shade, it being one of the unwritten laws of Livery that the Overcoat should match the cloth lining of the carriage; needless, however, to state, this is very often ignored.

The quantity of material required for cutting these coats is on an average 2¾, and they should be cut without wheal pieces to the skirts. A Diagram showing how this is done appears in the "Cutter's Practical Guide to Cutting all kinds of Livery Garments". And now a few words on

The Cutting.

Experience teaches us that garments cut from thick material, such as Devon, will not fit into the hollow of the back as readily as thinner makes, consequently we only come in ½ an inch from construction line at waist, there is only 1 inch taken out between back and sidebody, and only ¾ inch under the arm; 3½ inches will be found sufficient to allow over chest and waist taken over the vest. In making the first sweep add fully ½ an inch to the front shoulder measure as taken on the figure, but only add ¾ inch to this when making the second sweep; and add ½ an inch to the over shoulder measure when making the third sweep. The sewing-to edge of the lapel is cut by the front edge of forepart, the width at top and bottom being usually 2½ inches, with the outer edge straight or nearly so. The skirt is cut as follows: A is 3½ inches below waist seam; A, 9, is drawn at right angles, 9 is 9 inches from hip, from which point come out 1, and draw line through from top, add on ½ inch of round. Come up from line A ¾ at underarm seam and continue across to the waist as shown. Allow about ¾ inch for fulness, and get the run of front by squaring from B * and waist line front, B * is 3½ inches below the waist line.

Allow 1 inch to the length desired, and make the front the same length as the back. Carefully test the forepart to see the waist seams correspond both sides, and complete as per Diagram. The collar is of the Prussian type, a Diagram of which appears on Plate 9. To those who cater for the Livery trade we especially commend our new work on Livery Garments. It is a most comprehensive work, dealing with every kind of dress and undress garment worn by Livery servants; the price is 10/-. It is a companion work to the present one.

JUVENILE OVERGARMENTS.
Plate 19.

Long before the boy is ready for knickers, &c., the tailor is called upon to supply him with an Overgarment, and as this requires many special features, we have deemed it worthy of a place in this work. The earliest demand is the Kilt Overcoat which, as its name signifies, is a garment intended for wear over the frocks and skirts worn by very little boys. The boy at the age of 2½ or 3 years is generally short bodied, short necked, corpulent and erect, as compared with the adult figure. The necessary variations of shape for these disproportions have been made in the Diagram, which, if reproduced by the ordinary inch tape to the dimensions given, will fit a boy of 22 breast and 23 waist. The measures being taken over the frock. We consider it equally important to take the direct measures for juveniles as for adults; as the juvenile is seldom proportionate, and these measures if taken with care will provide for all variations of attitude and form of the shoulders, the disproportion of the waist being provided for by the omission of a fish and taking out no suppression between forepart and back at sideseam. In order to get sufficient spring over the

lower part to go over the skirt nicely, it will be necessary to spring out below the waist of both sides of back, and the sideseam of forepart. The plan followed in this case is to come in 6 inches from the waist point as at 10¼, and drop 1 or 1¼ inches and draw the part below this at right angles to 10¼ 1. Repeat this process at sideseam, which will give enough spring suitable for the majority of children.

It will be noticed there is only 2½ inches allowed over the breast, that quantity being sufficient, as the breast measure would be taken outside the frock worn. The Prussian collar, the cape and sleeves, are all produced on the same lines as are laid down elsewhere, so we need not again repeat these. Our illustration shows the front finished with a fly, but there is no reason why it should not be made to button through, or be double breasted if the customer so desires it. The buttons on the D.B. can be shifted forward as the lad grows, but it will be found his limbs will increase in length more rapidly than in size, so that the sleeves will be too short, long before the garment is too small in the chest; it is thus desirable to leave a good turn up at the bottom of sleeve.

The fly front is supposed to hide the wear of the button holes, but this is a small point, and is hardly to be noticed in making the choice of style, still this may be enough to turn the balance in favour of this choice.

The Austrian.

On this Diagram we have a more manly type of Overcoat, and one that looks smart and gentlemanly on a boy when he first dons suits. It is usually made to come to just above the knee, fastens up the front with a row of buttons hidden under a row of fur up to the neck; or it is ornamented with braid in the style shown on our Diagram, which forms the method of fastening the fronts. A reference to the Diagram will show this garment is cut quite on the same principle as for the adult, the check measures working all that is necessary in the shoulders, and the omission of the fish providing for the disproportion of waist. It may be useful to our readers to have a scale of proportionate measures for boys, and so we give our table of sectional measures a place in this page, and in it will be found the relative measures of the various parts of the average type of figure from 24 to 50 breast.

Gentlemen's Scale.

For Chesterfield, Morning Coat & Lounge

| Chest | Waist | Scye Depth | Lounge | | Morning Coat | | Across Back | Full Length Sleeve | Across Chest | Front Shoulder | Over Schoulder |
			Nat. Waist	Length	Fas. Waist	Length					
24	24	6¼	11¾	20			5⅛	19½	5¼	9½	12¾
26	25	6¾	13	22			5½	22½	5¾	10	13⅝
28	26	7¼	14	24			5⅞	25	6¼	10½	14¼
30	27	7¾	15	26			6⅛	27½	6¾	11	14¾
32	28	8¼	16	28	18	31½	6½	30	7¼	11½	15½
34	30	8⅝	16½	28½	18½	32	6⅞	31	7⅝	12	16¼
36	32	9	17	29	19	32½	7¼	32	8	12½	17
38	34	9⅜	17¼	29½	19¼	33	7⅝	33	8½	13	17¾
40	37	9¾	17¾	30	19¾	33½	8	33½	9	13½	18½
42	39½	10⅛	18	30½	20	34	8⅜	33½	9½	14	19¼
44	42	10½	18¼	31	20¼	34	8¾	34	10	14½	20
46	46	10¾	18½	31½	20½	34½	9	34	10½	15¼	21
48	50	11	18½	32	20½	34½	9¼	34	11	16	22
50	54	11¼	18½	32	20½	35	9½	34	11½	16¾	23

Length of Frock coats about 3 inches longer than Morning coats; Length of Chester 3 inches longer than Frock Coats.

Youths Overcoats

Can scarcely be said to have many distinguishing features from men's. They are generally cut to the easy side and are for the most part plain in style, though of recent years the Caped Chesterfield has been equally worn by youths and men, whilst sometimes orders will arrive for a Youth's Inverness. These, however, are exceptional.

The rules we have already laid down will work equally well for the youth as for the adult, so that it is unnecessary for us to dwell further on the requirements of the youth, the only special features to be found in him being a tendency to be long in the body and limbs, and sometimes a tendency to stoop, but the measures will indicate this in the usual way.

ECONOMICAL LAYS.
Plates 20 and 21.

The importance of a knowledge of the best way the garment can be taken from the cloth after the pattern has been cut, is so obvious, that a work of this class would be incomplete without some reference being made to it. We therefore give two illustrations. The one shows how to take an ordinary Fly Front Chesterfield out of about 2 yards of 56 inch faced material, with facings going right through the shoulder. This cannot fail to be useful alike to the novice and the experienced cutter. It will show the novice how the various parts are to be placed on the material so that it shall not be unduly biassed; it further shows the inlays it is advisable to leave when the cutter is engaged in the average bespoke trade, as well as the details of flaps, fly, pitch of sleeves, &c., these should be marked on the cloth for the workman's guidance. The experienced cutter will doubtless be fully acquainted with such details, but he will find the illustration useful in showing how to take the garment out of the least material to the best advantage.

For large sizes the position of the facings and undersleeve must be changed, and a slightly longer length will then be required, with that exception this lay may be followed for all sizes. The second lay shows how to take a

Caped Ulster

Out of about 3 yards of 56 inch Tweed, without a face or pile on it, several of the parts being reversed. We have followed this plan, as the majority of garments of this class are made from unfaced goods, such as Cheviots, Harris Tweeds, &c.

The facings are taken through the shoulder. This necessitates piecing, but there is sufficient for this as indicated by our lay.

Variations in either the length of coat or length of cape will, of course, necessitate an increase in the quantity required, but as a guide for fixing this our readers cannot do better than reckon twice the length of the coat and the length of the cape — thus twice 46 (the length of the Ulster) is 92, add 20 (the length of the Cape) 112, and 3 yards of material reckoning 37 inches to the yard equals 111 inches. These two lays must be taken as representative of the plan followed for all such garments. The cutter should mark out the entire garment, plan facings, collar, flaps, &c., before he commences cutting, it being a very extravagant method of cutting one piece before the whole garment has been planned.

Average Quantities.

To assist our readers in fixing the amount required for the various garments we append the following list, which will doubtless be found of service.

The average quantity of 56 inch material for a

36 breast Chesterfield is 2 yards.

36 breast Covert Coat is 1¾ yards.

36 breast Caped Overcoat is 3 yards.

36 breast Livery Overcoat is 2¾ yards.

36 breast Scarboro' and Long Cape is 2½ yards.

36 breast Inverness is 2½ yards.

36 breast Cassocks is 6 yards (28 inches wide.)

The Inverness wing may be taken out without a wheal piece by opening the material and taking the two wings and the two backs or the one *whole* back from the width. The skirts of Frock Overcoats and Box Coats are got without wheal pieces by folding the skirt over and placing the double edge of pattern to the crease of material. When cutting out with the material open in this way, great care is necessary to avoid cutting two for one side, as the right is just the reverse of the left; the best guide the cutter can have is to see that they face each other when cut out. It may be important to some, that we add here a few remarks on

Inlays.

These are necessary in bespoke garments, though they are found in some respects an evil, as they allow the workman scope to vary from the true lines, and whenever they are left on hollow seams there is a tendency to contract that part. Hence the cutter should aim at limiting them as much as possible, and to confine them where practicable to round seams. As an example, an inlay should never be left down the forearm of sleeve, when it can as easily be left on the hindarm, it is also better to leave it on the topside sleeve than the under, for the reason that if utilized it would carry the hindarm seam further under instead of bringing it more into prominence. The inlay left down the sideseam of forepart is a valuable one, but it is necessary to stretch it at the hollow of waist, so as to avoid contraction when the seam is opened. This same rule applies to the inlay left at the gorge, and under any circumstances we should not let this be more than inch from the neck point, as it will be very seldom used when working by this system — at least that is the result of the observations we have found in practical experience.

Our attention is occasionally directed, through the trade press and other sources, to the revival of some old style of garment or idea, such as we will now illustrate. We therefore use the term novelty on account of their exceptional character. Some firms are glad of such ideas for advertising purposes; but it is a question whether the return they receive for orders for these specialities pays them the cost of advertising.

The Seamless Overcoat is a good specimen of this type, and is found a puzzle to novices in the trade. It has neither back seam, sideseam, or shoulder seam. The indispensable join, as our illustration shows, comes across the breast pocket, of which there are generally a couple, the parts beyond, at front and scye, being hidden by seaming and rantering, or stoting, or fine drawing, according to the material. S at the top of Diagram joins J at the front of forepart. M joining in like manner to I. The easiest method of cutting is to take the pattern of a Chesterfield a size smaller than the customer would usually require. Cut the upper part of the forepart of the pattern above the breast pocket off, and grow it to the back as shown at B, C; then take the remaining portion of the forepart and grow it to the sideseam of back at D E. The breast pocket may either be arranged with a welt or flap, all that is necessary to note at I J is to allow whatever is necessary for seams at that part.

It must not be expected that this coat will fit closely at the waist, as it will not do so; but as a loose fitting Sack Overcoat it will pass muster. We recently saw one that had the forpart closed at G R and the upper part overlapping at F, this overlap was inserted as a wedge, and when nicely put is not seen. This had the effect of producing a smarter and closer fitting garment. This seamless idea is not new, it is to be found in most of the old works on cutting. Joe Hepple, in his work on cutting, gives a coat of this kind with sleeves and body all cut from one piece. Such arrangements may be clever, but they are of little practical value to the average cutter. Still orders do occasionally come for them, and our readers will doubtless be interested in knowing how to produce some of these trade wonders, which are after all only shams, they having seams in one place if not in the usual place; and where seams are omitted the garment lacks the character, style and comfort these are intended to produce

The next style we treat of is

The Four-in-Hand,

And this is undoubtedly a very practical garment. It is formed by a D.B. Reefer with long skirt arrangement to fasten round the waist under a belt and so give the appearance of an Ulster. Holes are left for the flaps of the hip pockets to come through, and these are secured in position by a hole and button under the tab. This is a very comfortable garment for travelling purposes, it being a very simple matter to take off the lower part and use it as a rug to wrap round the legs. The Reefer part is cut on the same lines as a D.B. Overcoat, the amount of overlap in front being regulated to taste, but usually 3 to 3½ inches would be about right. The spring over the hips and the deepening of the scye is done in the usual way for Overcoats. The only point of variation is in the length, unless it be decided to have slits at the sides, when the necessary facing must be allowed on the sideseam of the forepart in the usual way.

Draw line A B at right angles to the front; A to F is the same as 22 to 25; A to B is the same size as the back and forepart combined at waist line. B to C is 3½ to 4 inches; A * is also the same quantity; C D is squared from C *, D is 9 inches from C, and E is 1 inch out from D; draw line C K from C through E, and make up the length to taste, making it the same at front and back; C to A is drawn by a gradual hollow curve. In making up a belt is put on the top of this skirt so as to hide the top and give the appearance that it is all one garment. By its different combinations this may be used as a Reefer, an Ulster Overcoat, or a rug. Made from suitable material — by the class for whom it is intended — it should meet with a good demand. We give these two fancy styles as representing the unusual types of Overgarments introduced and advertised by so many firms in different parts of the country. They serve the purpose of showing how the principles we have laid down in the early portion of this work can be applied to all kinds of novelties, if the cutter is only possessed of some little tact and judgment.

CHESTERFIELD FROM LOUNGE PATTERN. Plate 23.

In the great rush of business at certain seasons in most of the large bespoke trades, any method of cutting whereby time and worry can be saved or avoided will be an acquisition to the cutter. The method we will now describe will meet this. The system of cutting by block patterns has many advantages; thus the time saved will be admitted by all. Worry and strain on the mind from the fact that it is easier to find the pattern desired when the number of blocks are reduced by one-half, although it must be admitted that certain deviations have to be made which require attention and thought. The method is as follows: — Take a

Model Pattern of Lounge

Two inches larger in the breast than the measure of the customer it is desired to cut for, that is presuming the chest measure has been taken over. the vest only, as advised in the early part of this work. Now proceed to lay down on the cloth, marking round it exact, extending it to the desired length, and leaving, on 1 inch to form the back tack, starting at 9 inches below the natural waist, and drawing the line from O through this point, as illustrated. This quantity is a good general one; it may be made a little more or a little less for very long or very short garments, but as a general quantity this will be found useful. We now turn our attention to the forepart, and the first thing we do is to add on ¾ inch at breast and 1 inch at waist in front, that is to produce the ordinary Fly Front style, varying these amounts according to the style of front desired. Mark round the gorge, as illustrated, being careful to keep it fairly well up at I; add ⅜ inch across the front shoulder from J to D, follow round the scye exact, and continue down the sideseam to the waist, below which point it should be sprung out over the hips either in the style previously described, of coming in 6 inches and down 1, and squaring, or of adding 1½ inches to the spring over the hips at the bottom of the lounge. These alterations are necessary to allow sufficient room in the skirts for walking purposes, and to give sufficient extra room in the shoulders to allow of its going over another coat. As regards the sleeve the principal variation is a little (say ½ inch) extra width added to the elbow and cuff at the hindarm. The relative length of back and front is found as previously described, whilst the same rules would hold good for the position of the pockets, and the other general details.

Before bringing this work to a close we will introduce a garment which, although not an Overcoat in the true sense of the word, yet has many features in common, and consequently we give it a place in these pages.

THE CASSOCK.
Plate 24.

This, as we presume everyone knows, is a clerical garment, though its use is not confined to clergymen. Choristers, vergers, &c., wear them, the former under their surplices, and the latter to cover the garments they are wearing.

There are many kinds of Cassocks: long Cassocks and short Cassocks, double breast and single breast, three-seam Cassocks, and Cassocks with sidebodies, plain Cassocks and Cassocks with capes; so it may be well to deal briefly with their various features. Cassocks generally are nothing more than a long three-seam garment, worn over the usual clerical under garments, and under the surplice; the most general form being that illustrated by the Diagram on Plate 24. It is cut with three seams, with box pleats arranged at the back, and sideseams; at the sideseam pleats pockets are inserted, and openings left through which the trouser pockets may be reached. The pockets are arranged so as to fall on either side of this pleat. The general rule as regards length is for the garment to reach to the seam of the heel of the boot behind, and the front, so that the wearer may walk with ease. It is invariably finished with a stand collar, the amount of opening in front being quite a matter of taste.

Of Cassock is much favoured by clergy of the old school, it is made double breasted and is illustrated on our Diagram sheet by the fine line beyond the front. It is cut on similar lines to the first mentioned, as far as the seams and pleats are concerned, but it is made to wrap well over the front, and often finished with a fly up the side. The fronts are often made reversible and are fastened at the neck with a cord.

A plaited belt, cincture, or similar appendage is invariably worn on this style of Cassock.

Then there is the short Cassock, which is really a combination of the apron and Cassock vest. The neck and front are fastened in the same way as we have just described. It is made up without sleeves, and the foreparts are intended to be reversible. A ribbon sash 4½ inches wide is now worn round the waist, tied with strings at the back. This is the Cassock worn by archdeacons, deans, bishops and archbishops, of the established church, other clergymen sometimes wear them when they desire to appear in full dress.

There is another kind of S.B. Cassock which is different from our Diagram, in that it is cut with sidebodies, after the style of a body coat, the waist seam being terminated at the sideseam after the style of the Paletot illustrated on another page. The waist is cut rather longer than for an ordinary body coat, and is made fairly easy fitting at the waist. One of the most important parts of a Cassock is the neck, and every care should be used to get it not only the right size, but to get the height of collar and the opening in front of the right style to suit your customer, and as may be imagined there is a great diversity of taste. Some Cassocks are finished with a cape extending to the elbows, but these are the exception, and are only used by the catholic clergy, and not by all of them.

The cuffs are sometimes finished with a gauntlet, but more often left plain. Buttons are placed up the front about 1¾ inches apart, which will make about 40 for a clergymen of average height, but this is also a matter of taste. Below the waist these are arranged so that only every other one buttons. They are generally lined to the hips with either Italian cloth or Silesia, the latter being quite as much used as the former.

The materials mostly used are Russell Cord and Serge, though alpaca and silk are also often used; silk is always adopted for the short D.B. Cassock or Bishop's apron we have described. Black is, of course, the colour, though it is not universal, violet and scarlet being occasionally used, though these colours must be looked upon as the exception rather than the rule.

The method of gauging the length of the Cassock is to take 10 inches off the full height; this is of great service when one is unable to measure the customer. Special care is necessary to avoid getting the neck too large.

The Cutting

Of these garments is more on the lines of a lounge in the shoulders, there being no additions to the measures as taken on the wearer. It is made fairly easy fitting at the chest, 2½ inches being allowed beyond the actual breast measure from back seam to breast line; but at the waist this should be increased to 3 or 3½ inches, as they usually fit easy at that part. The spring of the back pleats is got by coming out from point 20, 3 inches, and drawing a line straight through from point O at the top of back neck. The spring of the side is got by coming down 1 from the natural waist line as shown from 17 to 18 and squaring the side from 7, 18, and adding on 3½ inches to form the pleat, this same process at the side of foreparts as the Diagram fully illustrates.

In Conclusion

We would thank our readers for the liberal support accorded to the former parts of "The Cutter's Practical Guide", and in adding this to the list we trust it will be found worthy of study and consideration, and if our fellow craftsmen find in it a help to the performance of their various duties, we shall feel our labour has not been in vain.

Plates of Diagrams

ILLUSTRATING

 THIS WORK.

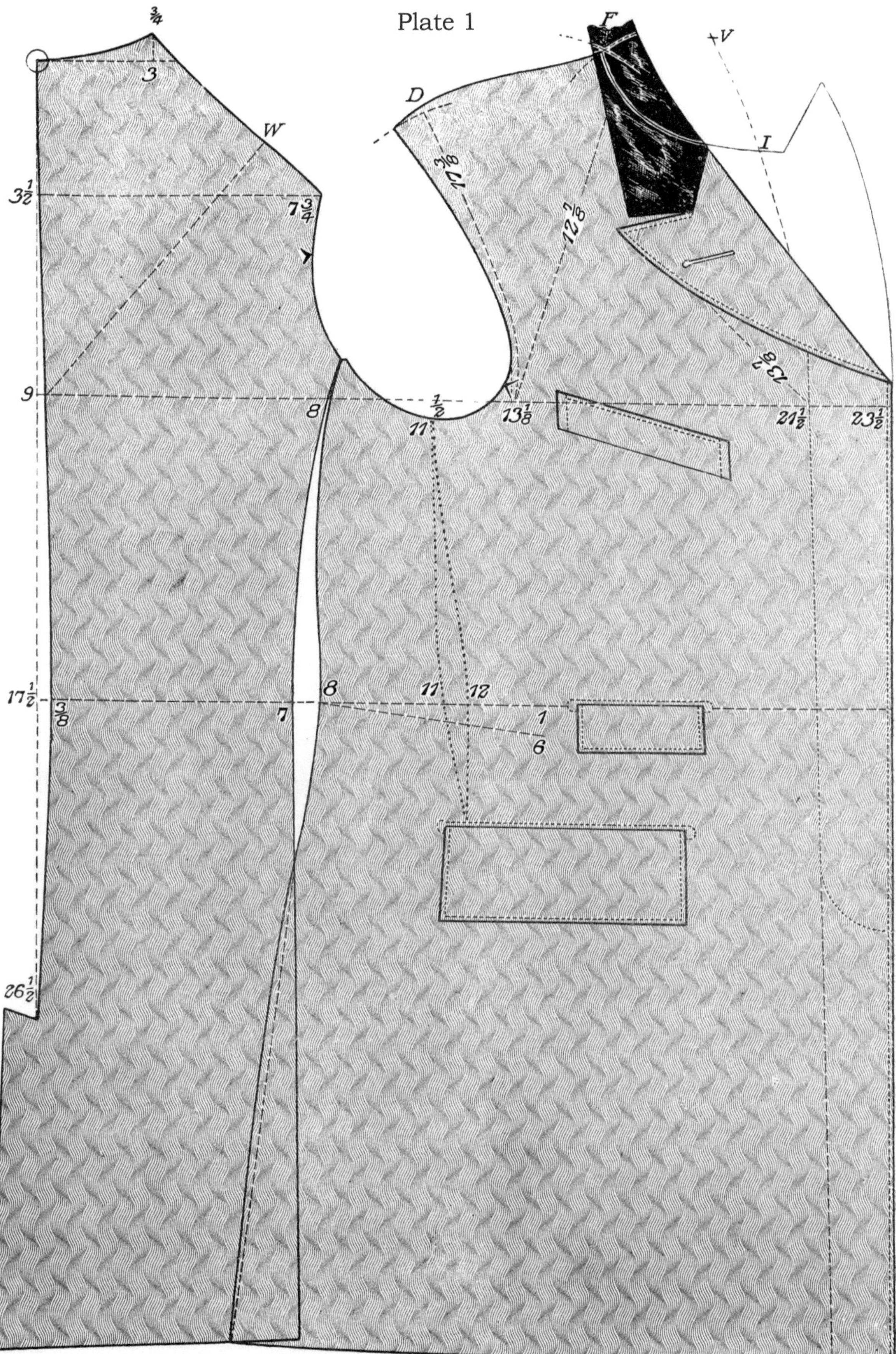

3/4
3
W
3 1/2
7 3/4
9
8
1/2
11
17 1/2
3/8
7
8
11
12
1
6
26 1/2
F
+V
D
I
17 3/8
12 1/8
13 3/8
13 1/8
21 1/2
23 1/2

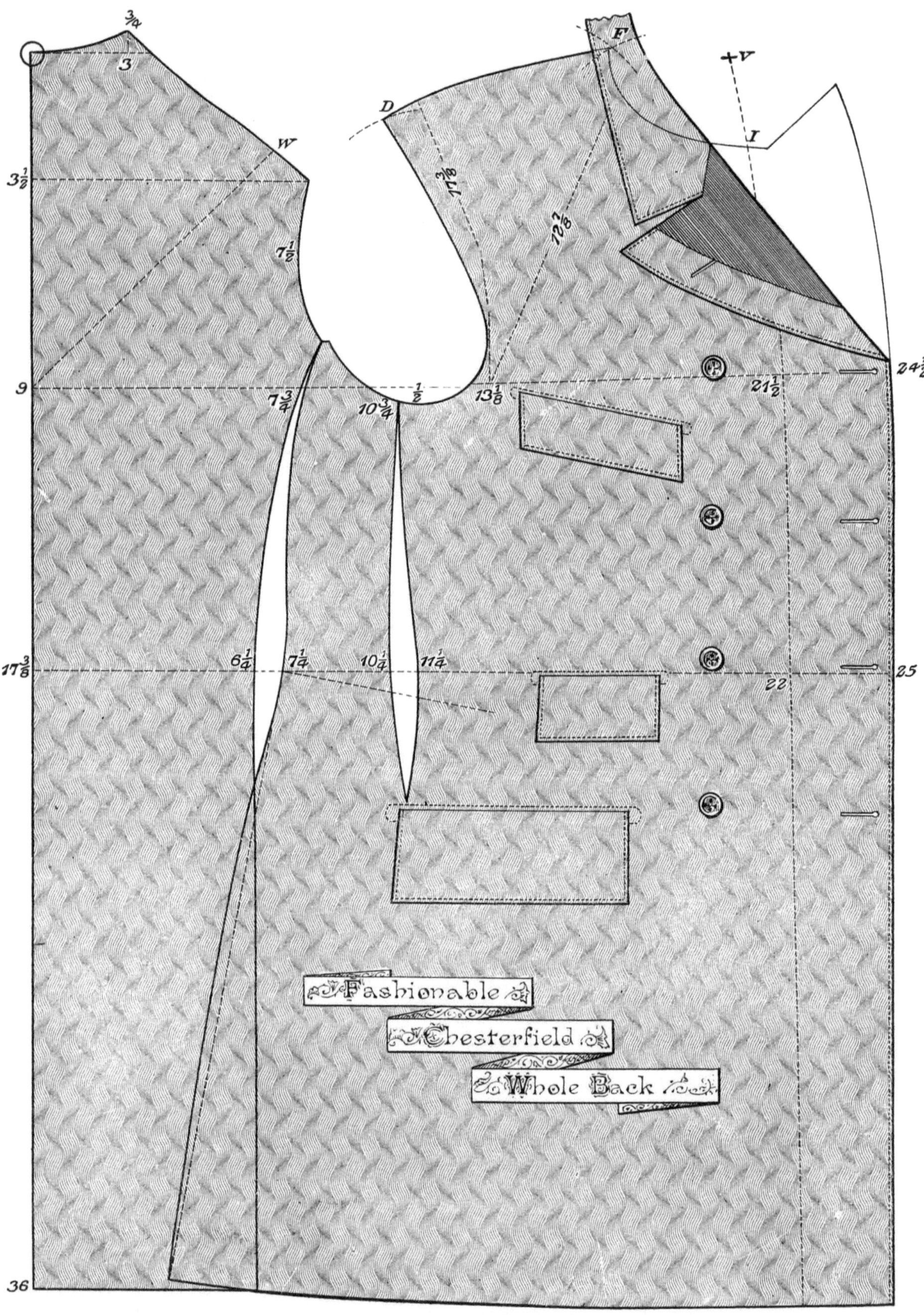
Fashionable
Chesterfield
Whole Back

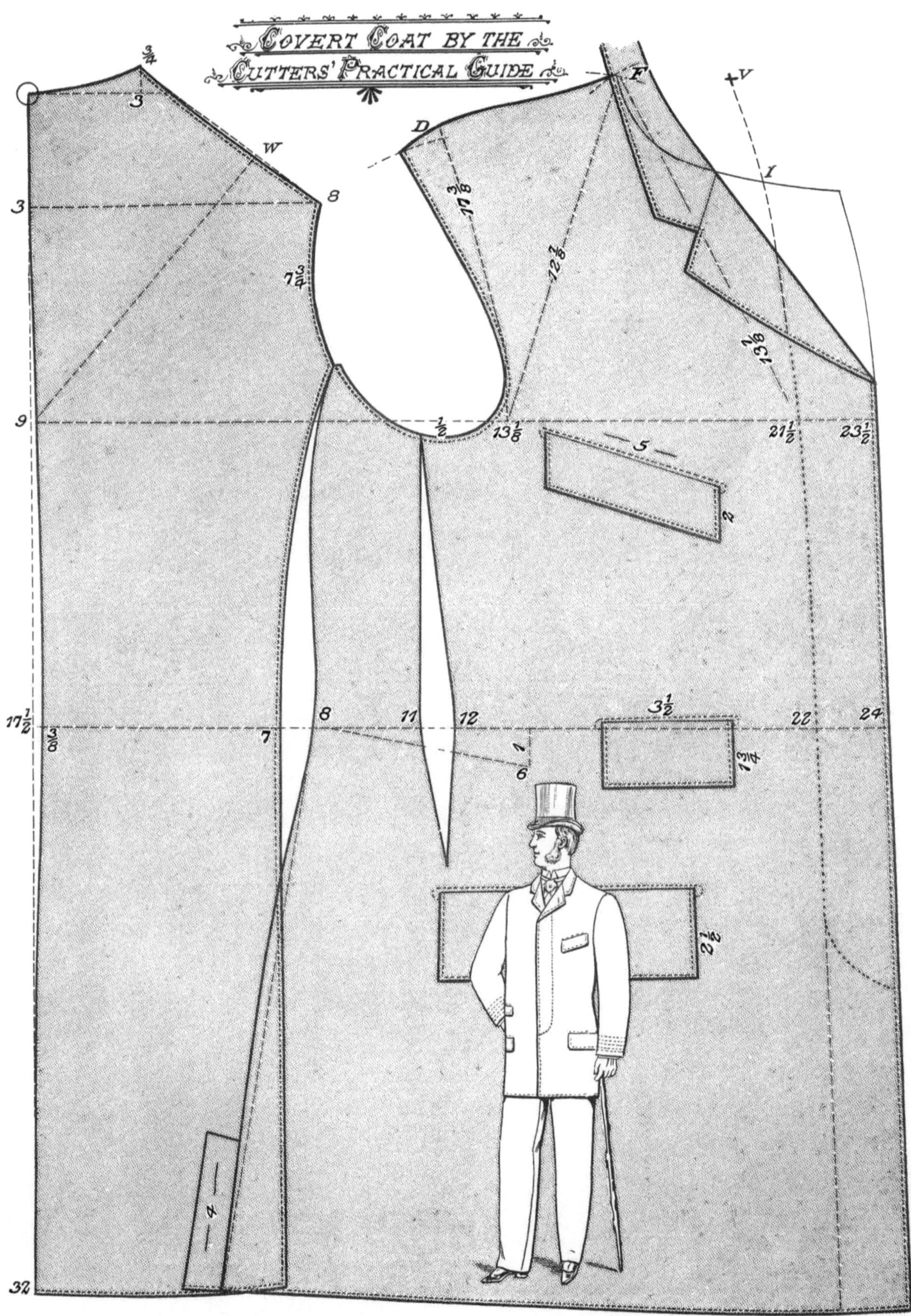

COVERT COAT BY THE
CUTTERS' PRACTICAL GUIDE
3/4
3
W
3
8
7 3/4
9
17 1/2
3/8
7
8
11
12
6
32
D
3 7/8
12 1/2
13 8/8
1/2
13 8/8
5
2
3 1/2
1 3/4
22
24
2 1/2
F
V
1
13 8/8
21 1/2
23 1/2

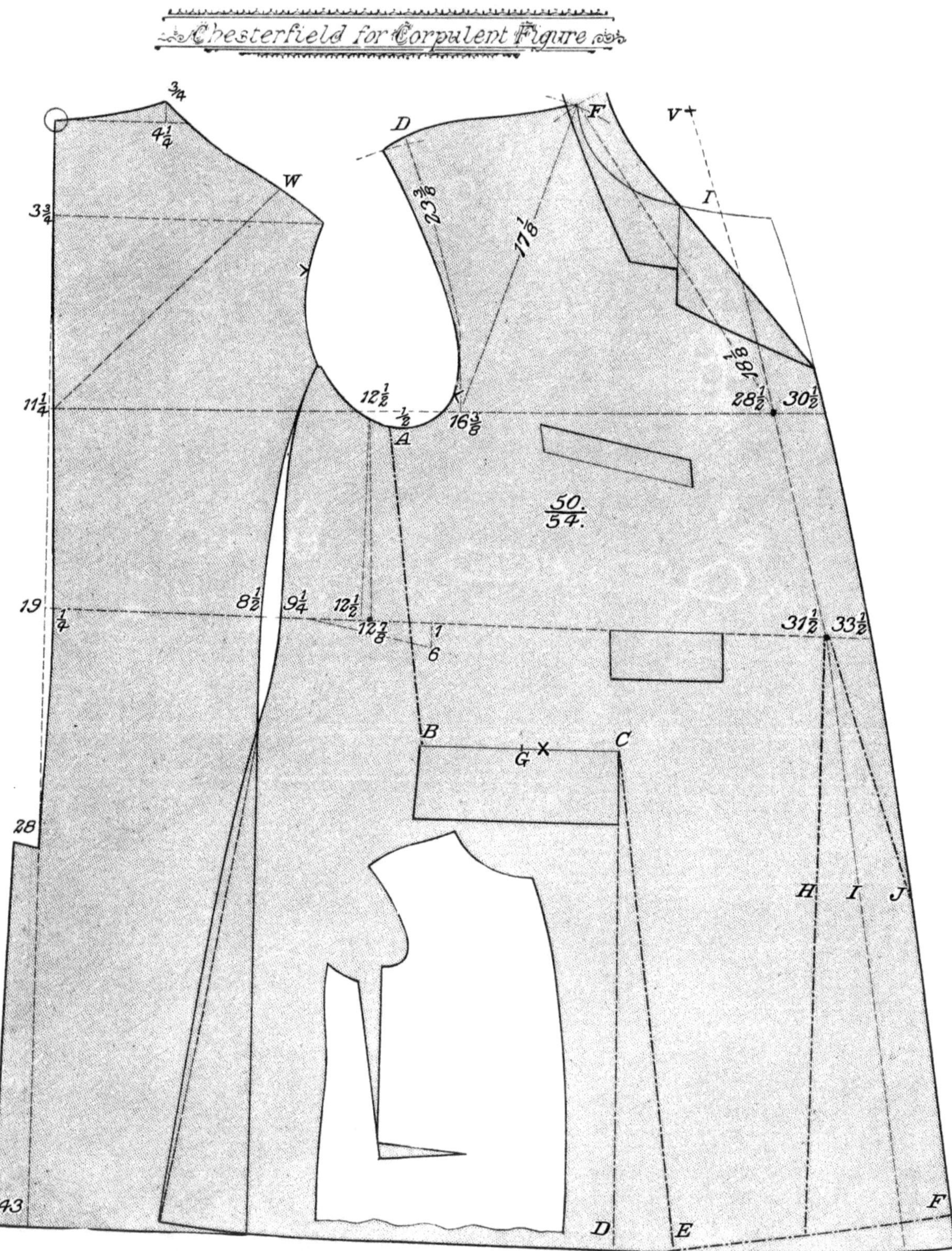
Chesterfield for Corpulent Figure
50.
54.

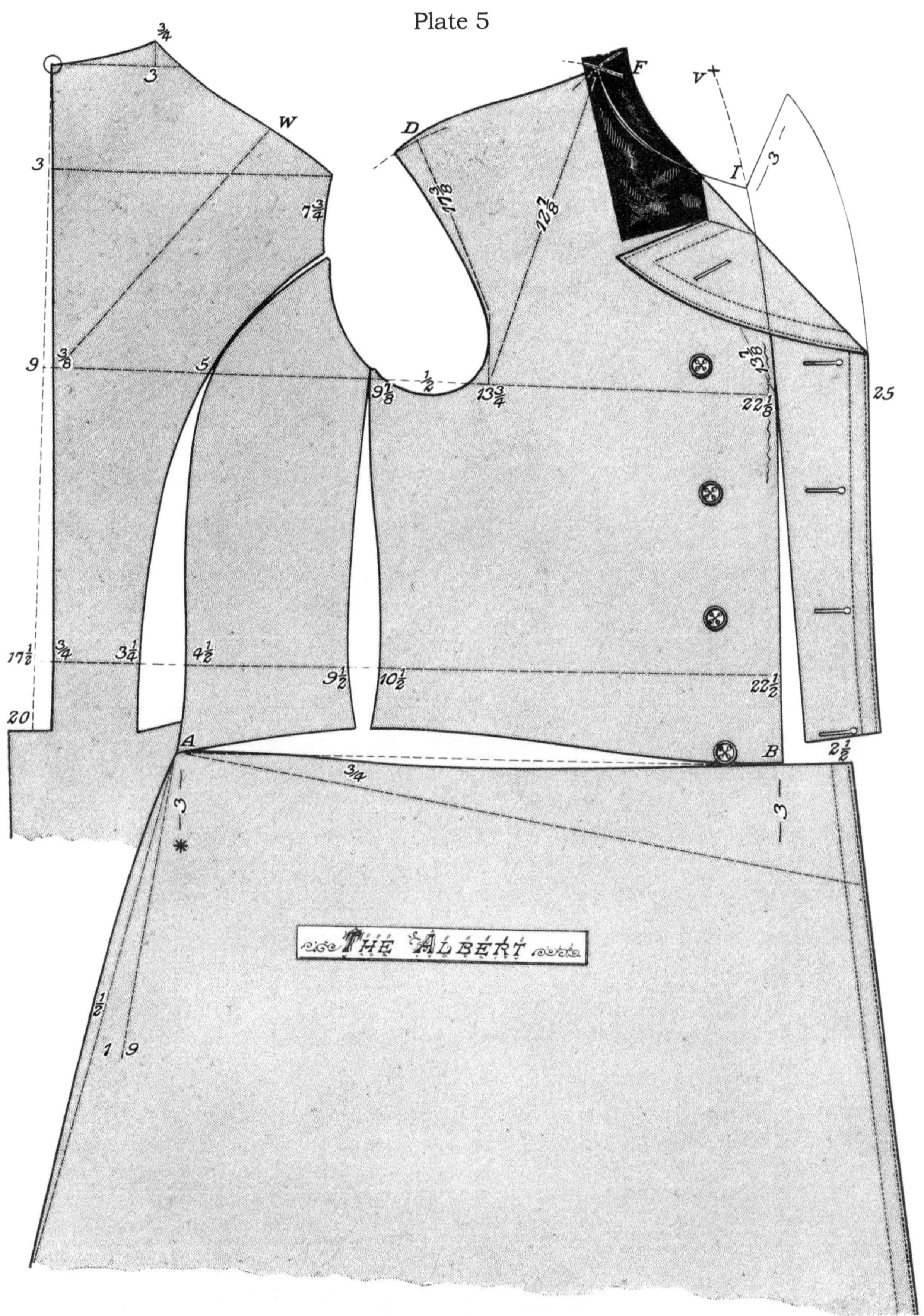
THE ALBERT

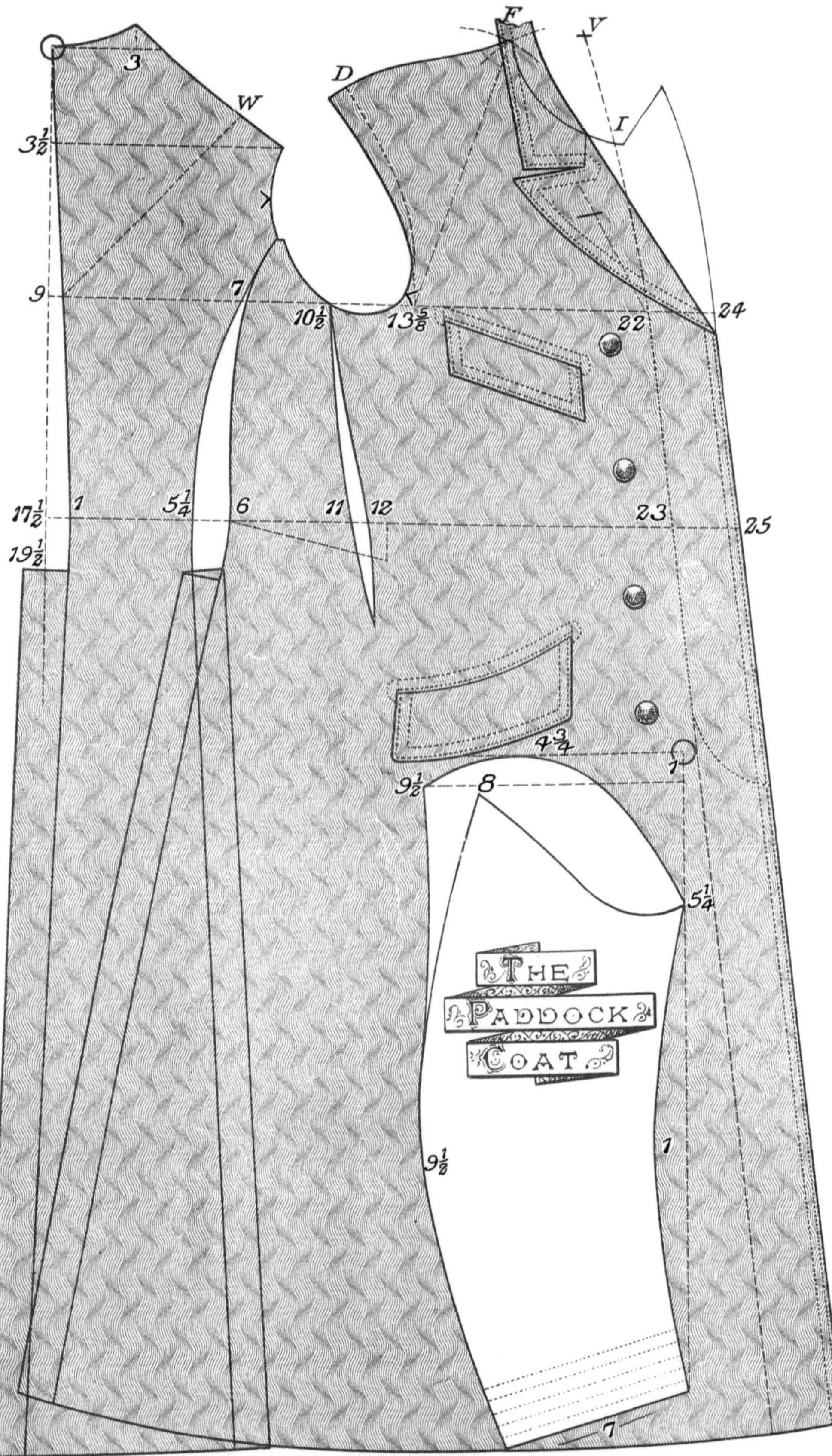
THE
PADDOCK
COAT

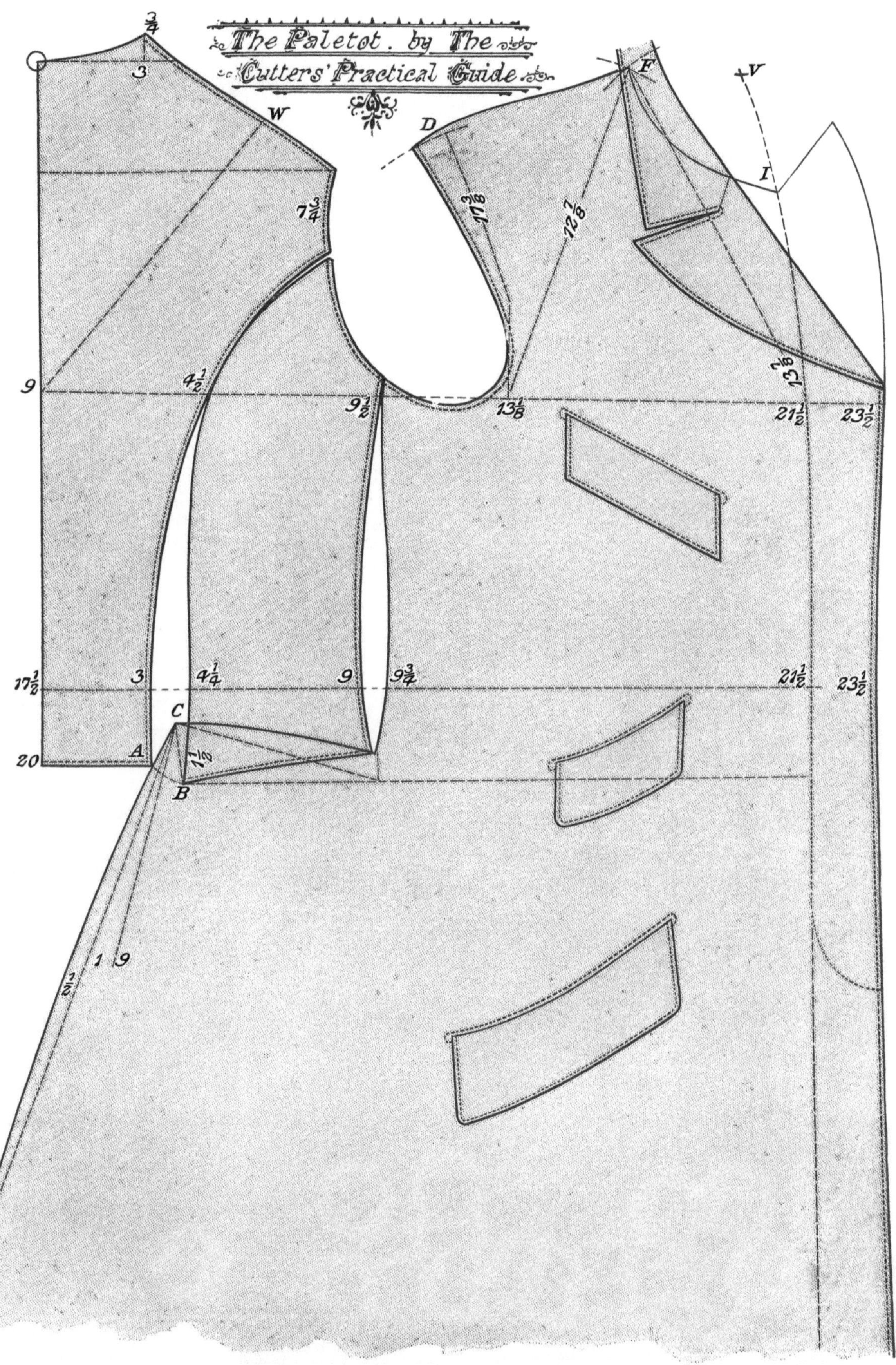
The Paletot. by The
Cutters' Practical Guide

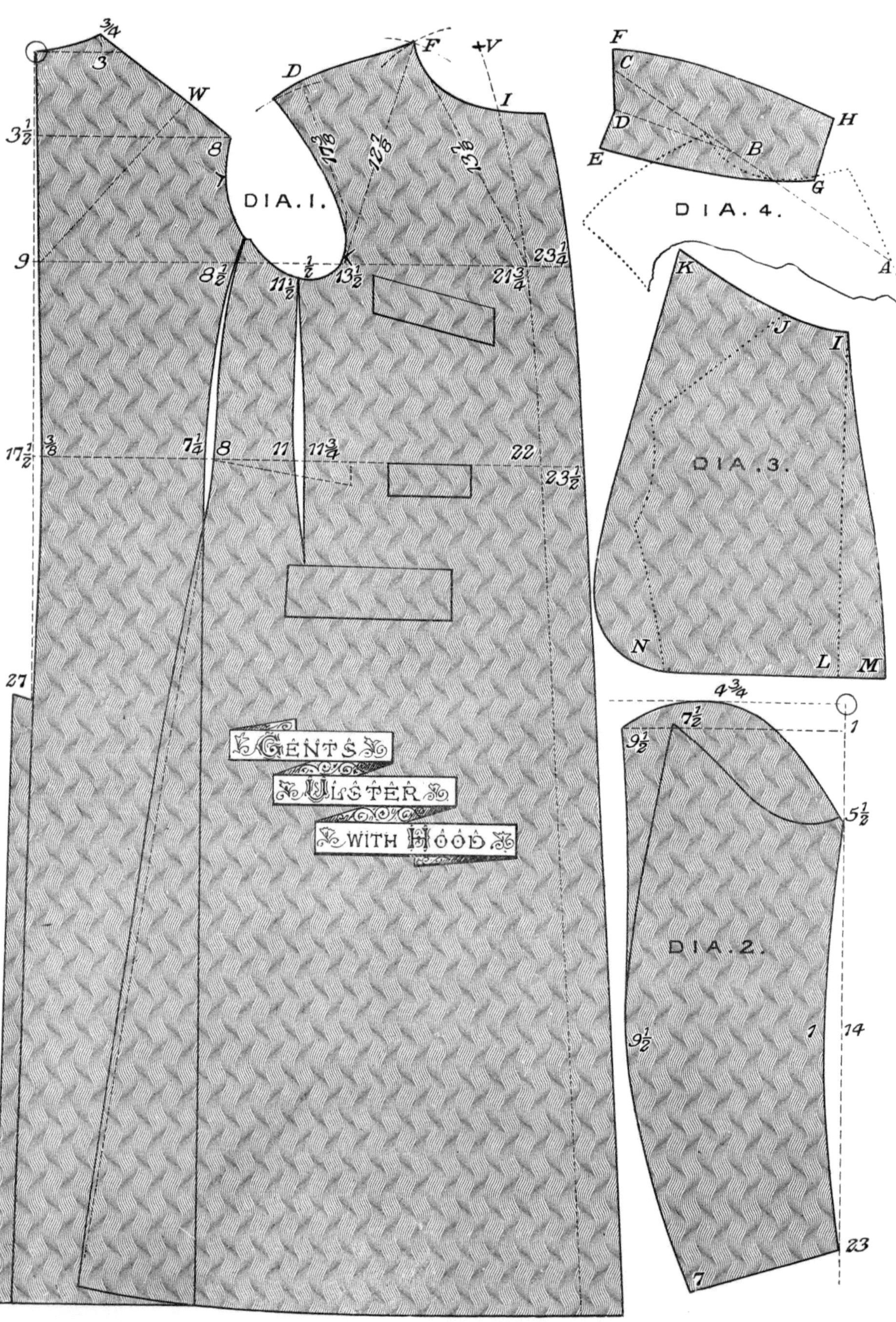
DIA. I.
DIA. 2.
DIA. 3.
DIA. 4.
GENTS ULSTER WITH HOOD

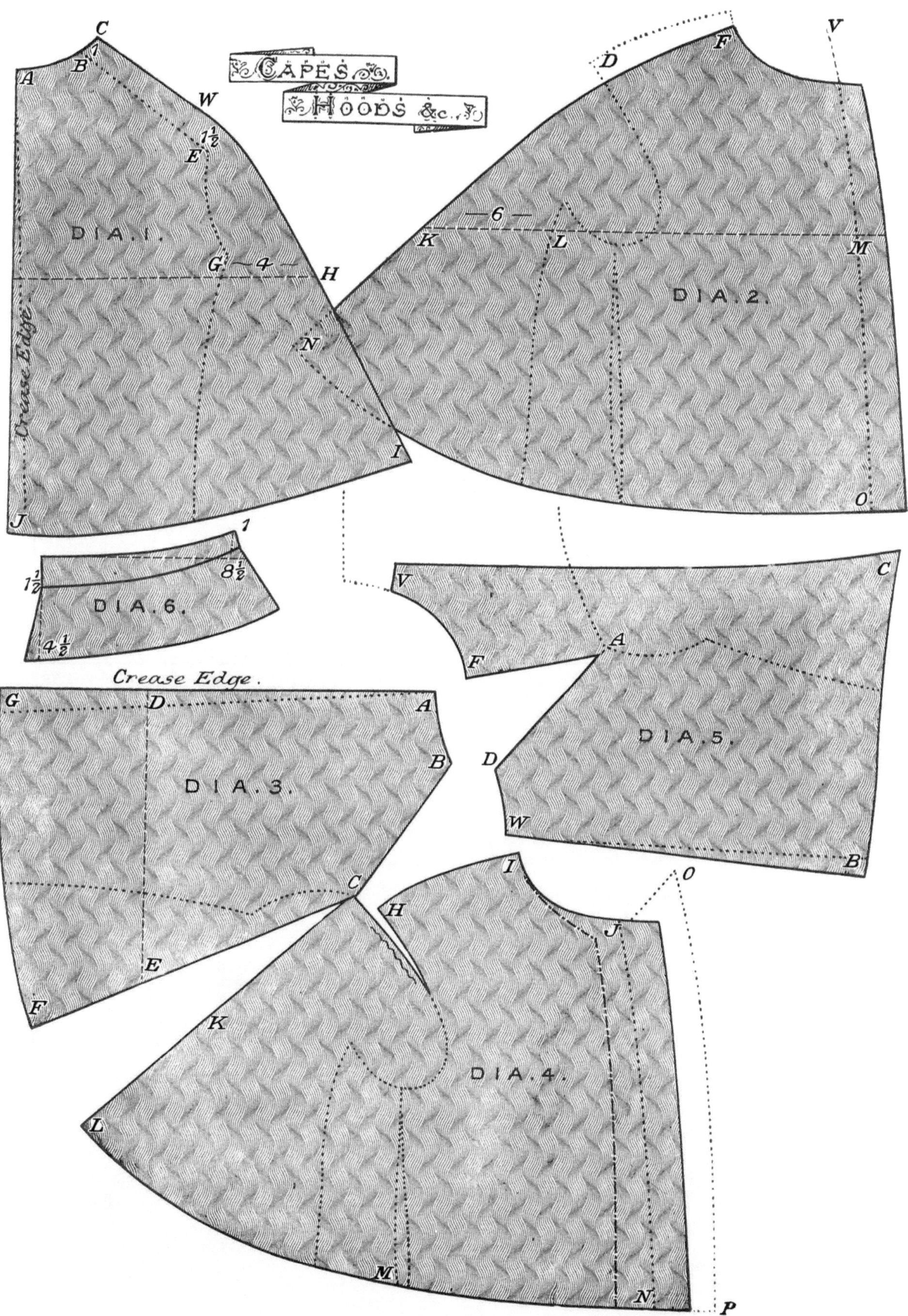
CAPES
HOODS &c.

C
B 1
A
W
E 1½
DIA. 1.
Crease Edge
G — 4 — H
N
J
I

D
F
V
K — 6 — L
M
DIA. 2.
O

1
1½
8½
DIA. 6.
4½

V
C
F
A
D
DIA. 5.
W
B

Crease Edge.
G D A
B
DIA. 3.
C
E
F

I
O
H
J
DIA. 4.
K
L
M
N
P

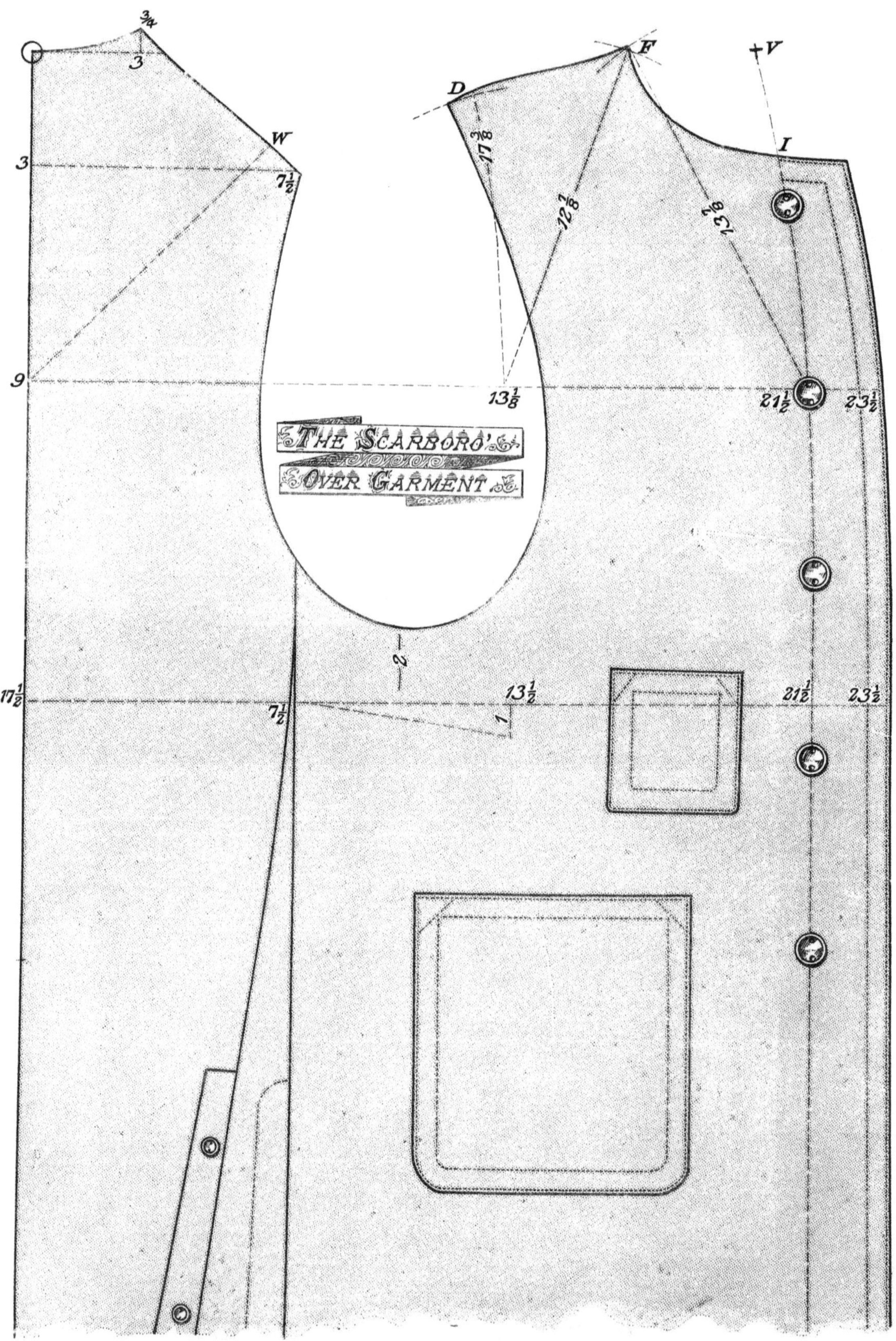

THE SCARBORO'
OVER GARMENT

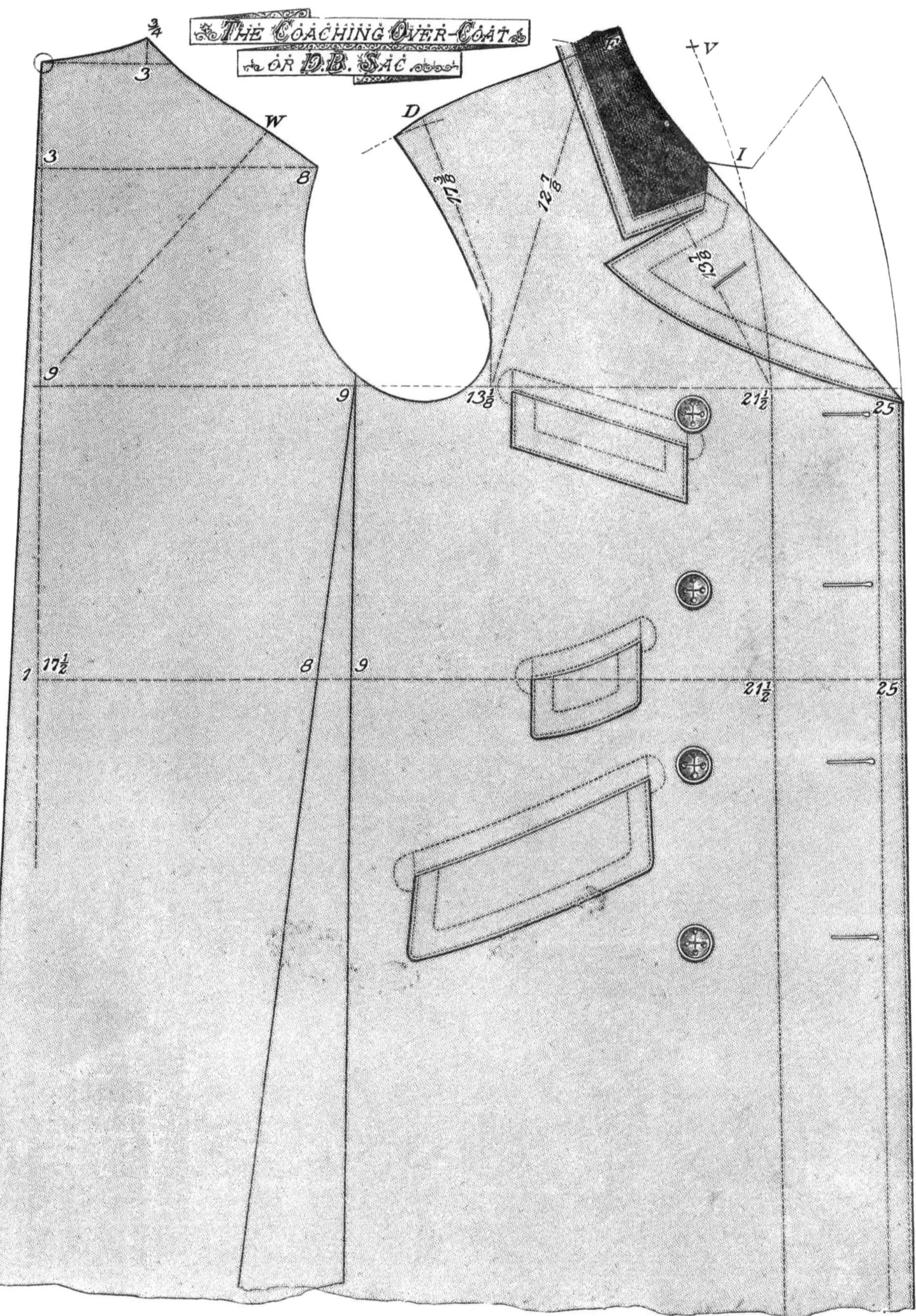
THE COACHING OVER-COAT
OR D.B. SAC.

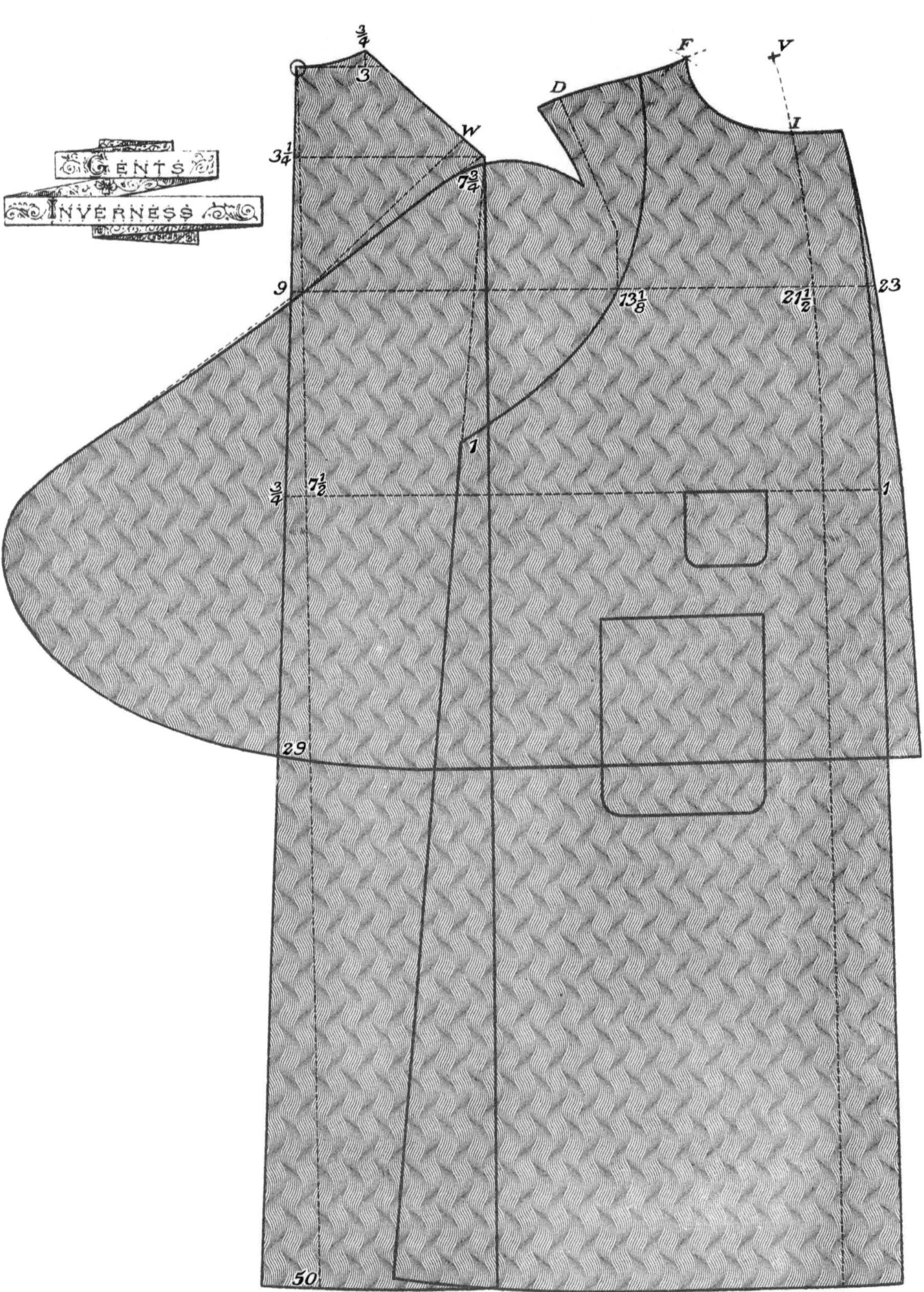

GENTS
INVERNESS
¾
3
W
3¼
7¾
9
1
¾ 7½
29
50
D
F
V
I
13⅛
21½
23
1

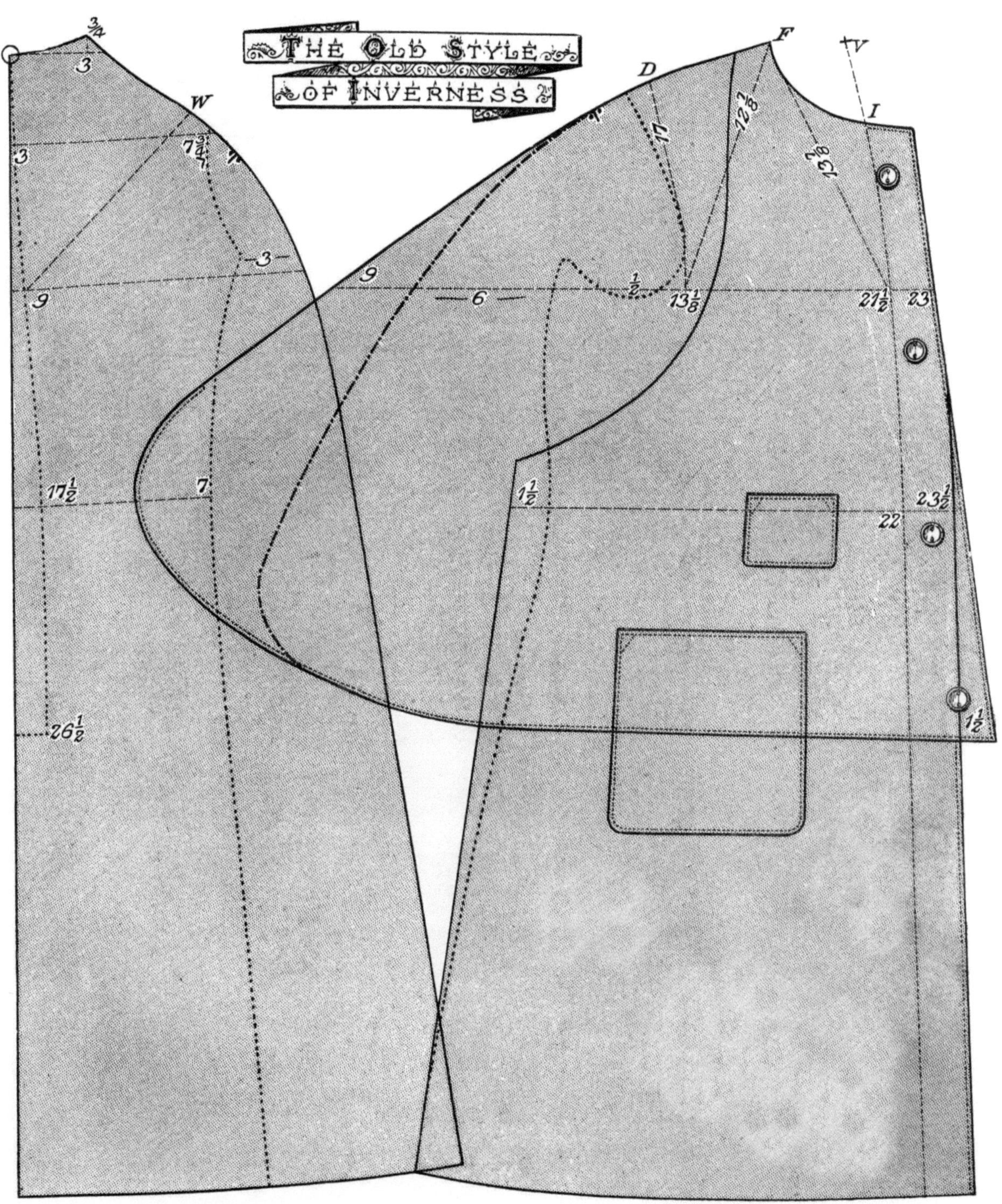
THE OLD STYLE OF INVERNESS
3/4
3
3
W
7 3/4
4
3
9
9
17 1/2
7
26 1/2
9
6
1/2
13 1/8
1 1/2
D
4
17
12 1/8
F
V
I
13 7/8
21 1/2
23
23 1/2
22
1 1/2

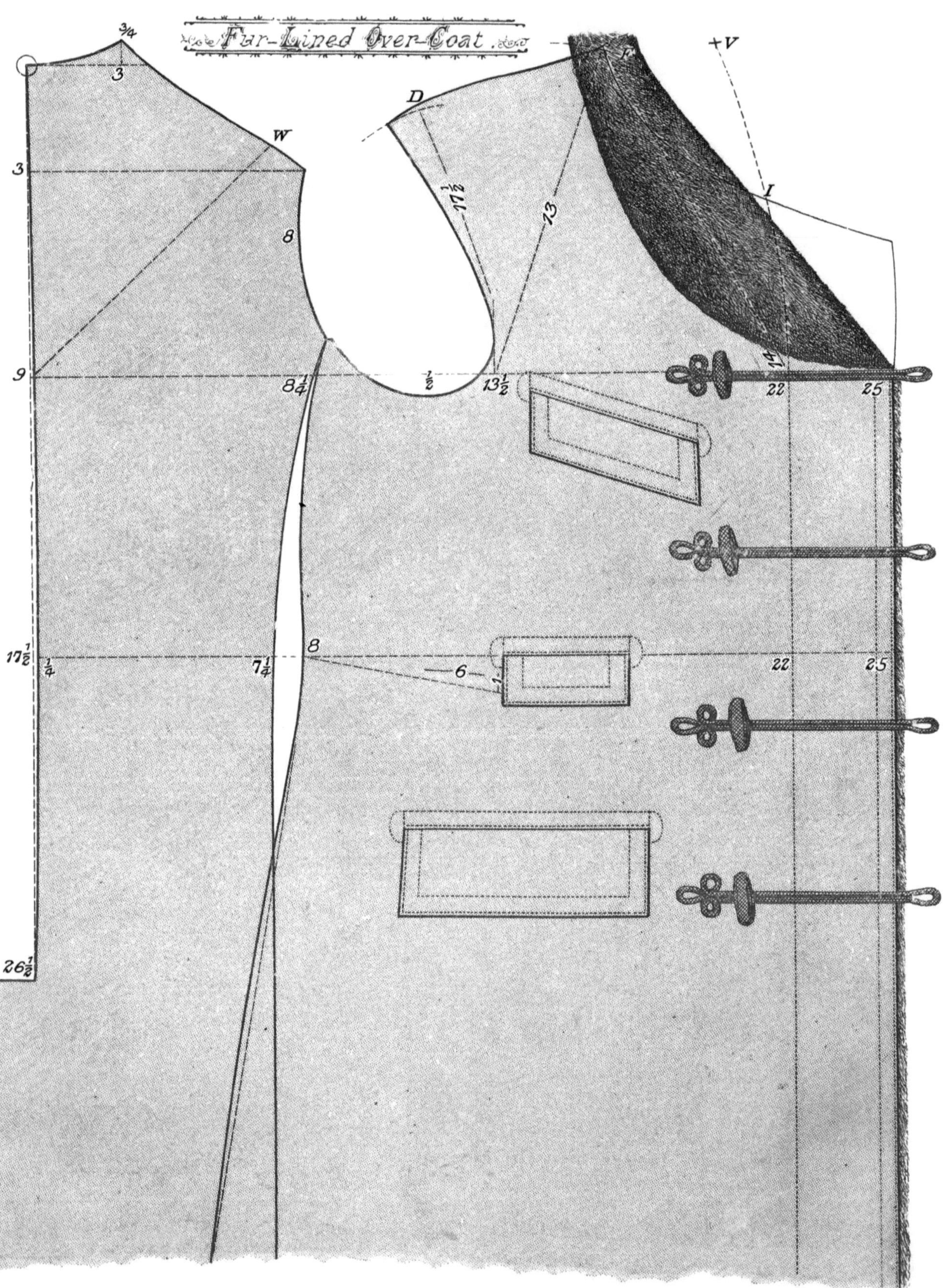
Fur-Lined Over-Coat.
3/4
3
W
8
9
D
17½
13
+V
F
I
8¼
⅜
13½
14
22
25
17½
¼
7¼
8
6
22
25
26½

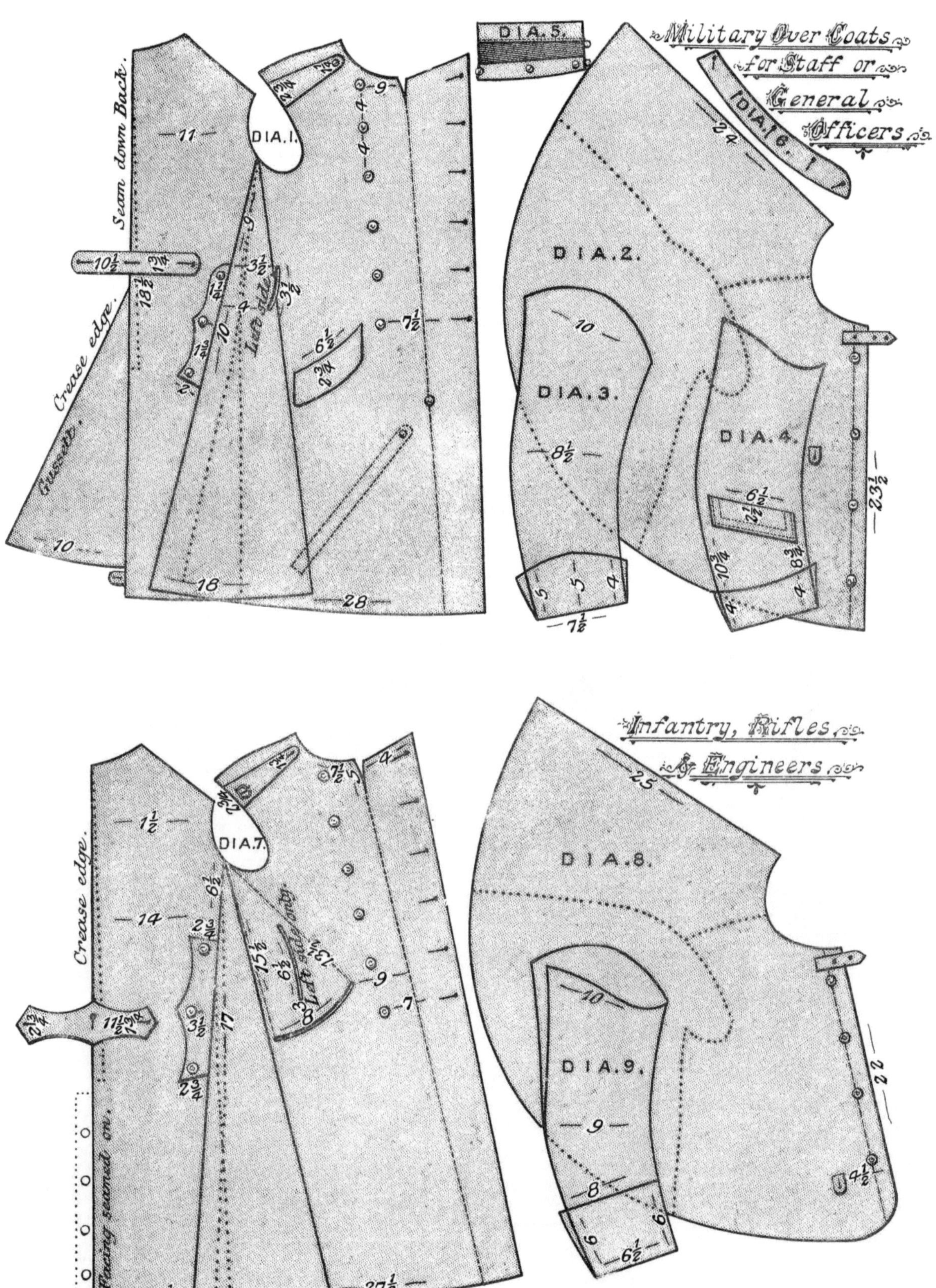

Military Over Coats
for Staff or
General
Officers
Infantry, Rifles,
& Engineers
Seam down Back.
Crease edge.
Gusset.
DIA.1.
DIA.2.
DIA.3.
DIA.4.
DIA.5.
DIA.7.
DIA.8.
DIA.9.
Facing seamed on.
Crease edge.
Left side.

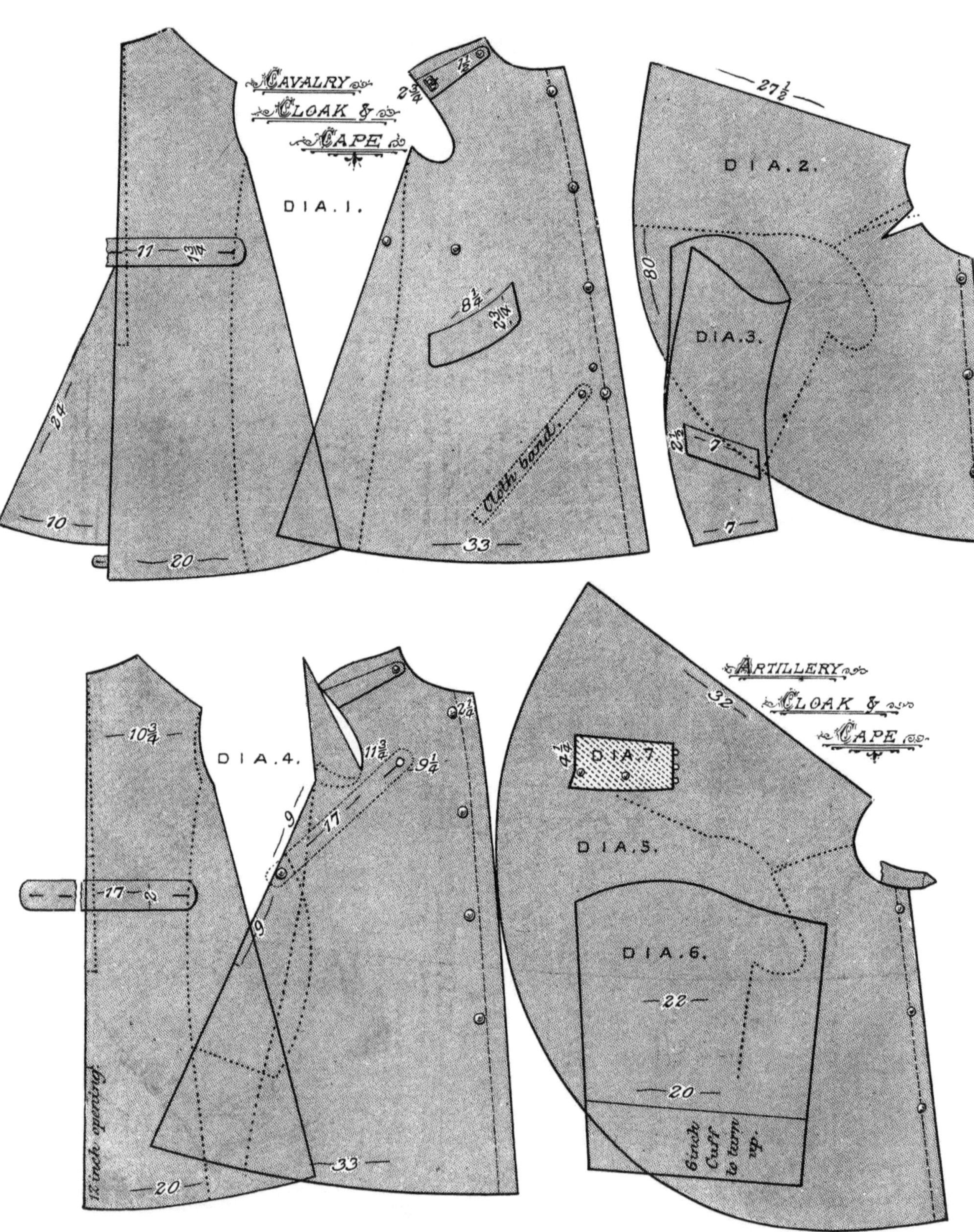
CAVALRY CLOAK & CAPE
DIA.1.
2¾
7½
11 — 1¾
24
8½
2¾
10
20
Cloth band.
33
DIA.2.
27½
30
DIA.3.
2½
7
7
DIA.4.
10¾
11¾
2¼
9¼
9
17
9
14 — 2
9
12 inch opening.
20
33
ARTILLERY CLOAK & CAPE
32
DIA 7
4½
DIA.5.
DIA.6.
22
20
6 inch
cuff
to turn
up.

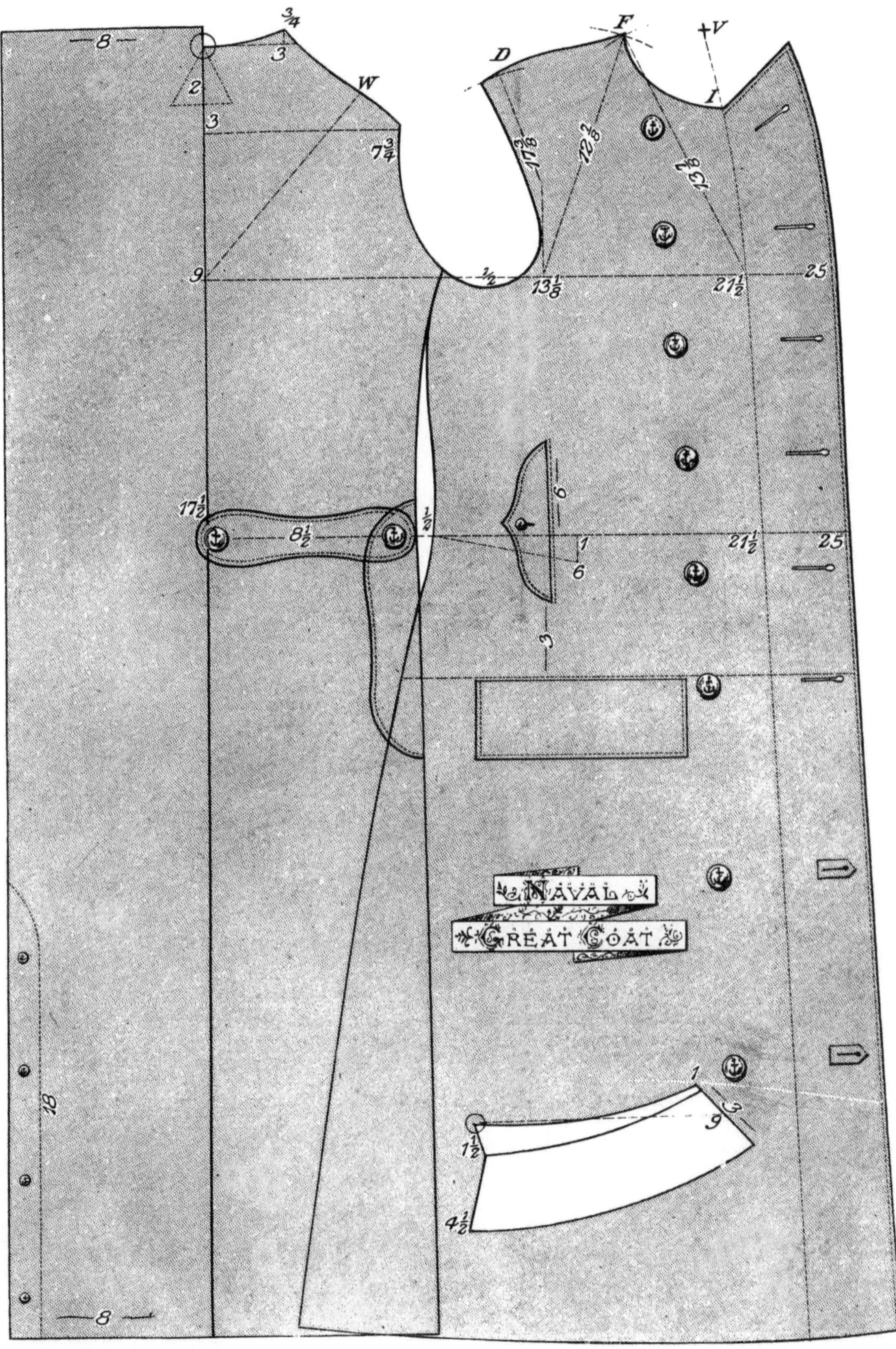
NAVAL
GREAT COAT

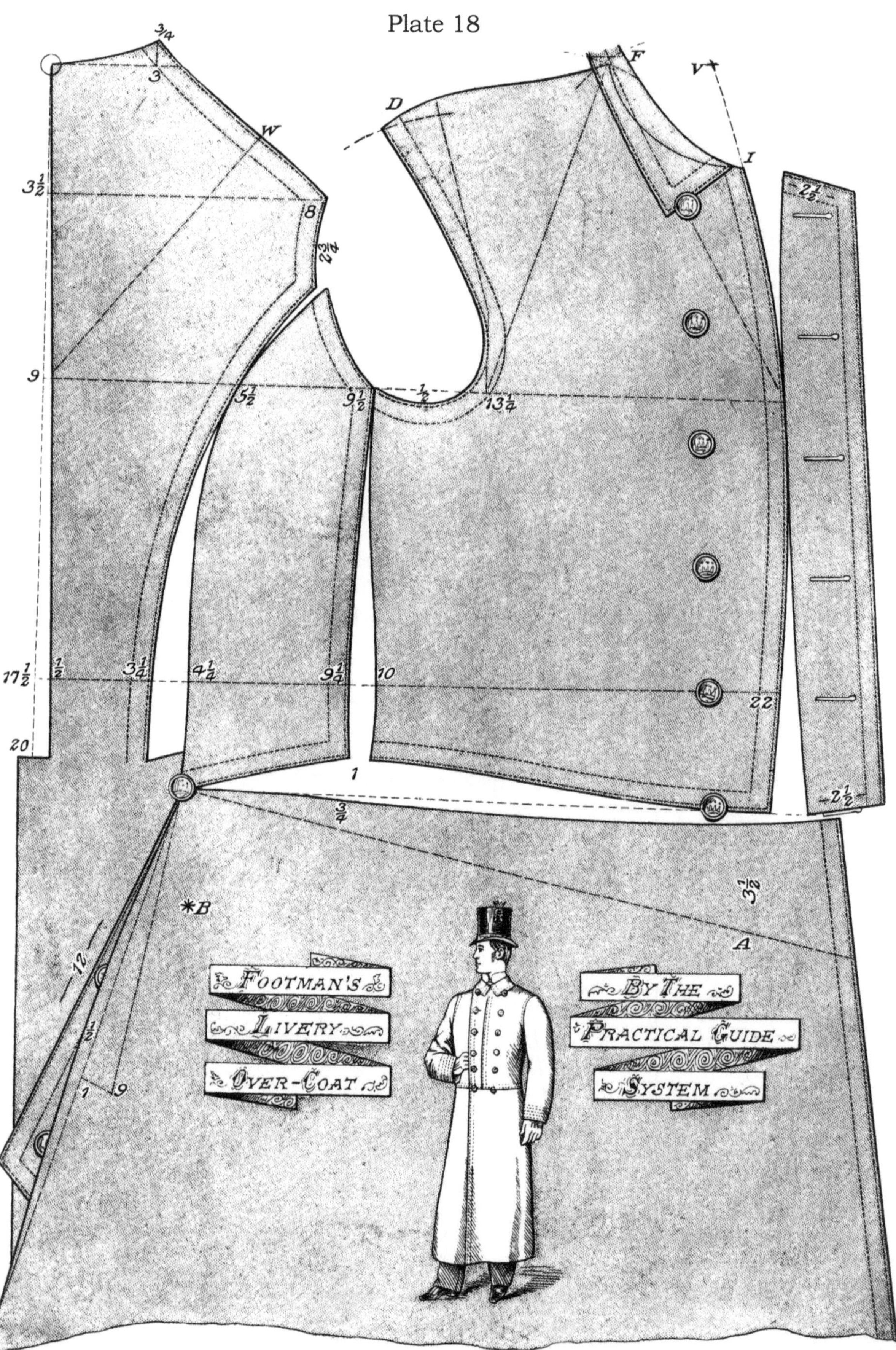
3/4
3
W
8
2 3/4
3 1/2
9
5 1/2
9 1/2
1/2
13 1/4
17 1/2
1/2
3 1/4
4 1/4
9 1/4
10
20
1
3/4
*B
12
1/2
1 9
D
F
V
I
2 1/4
2 1/2
22
3 1/2
A
2 1/2
FOOTMAN'S
LIVERY
OVER-COAT
BY THE
PRACTICAL GUIDE
SYSTEM

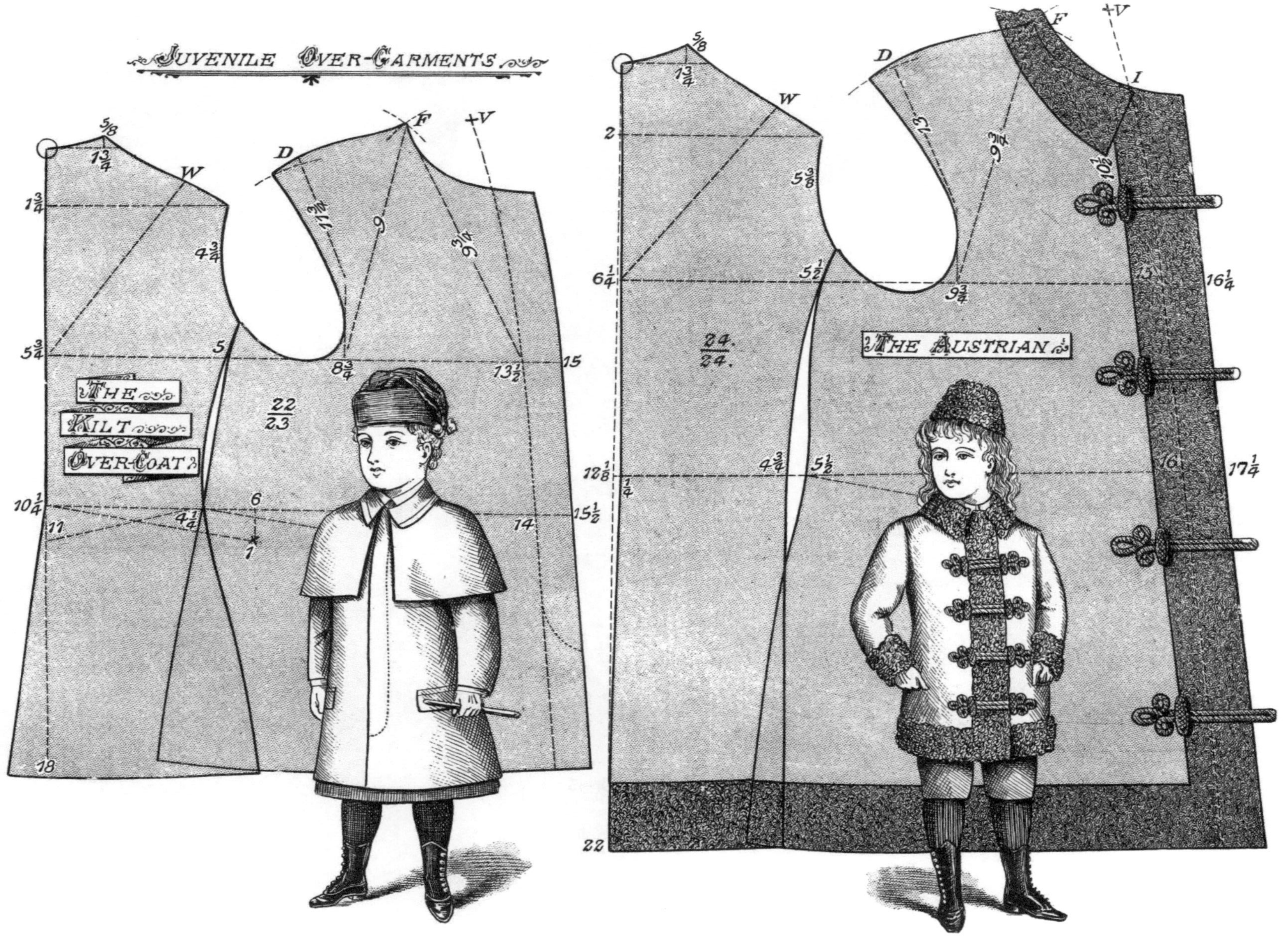
JUVENILE OVER-GARMENTS
THE KILT OVER-COAT
THE AUSTRIAN

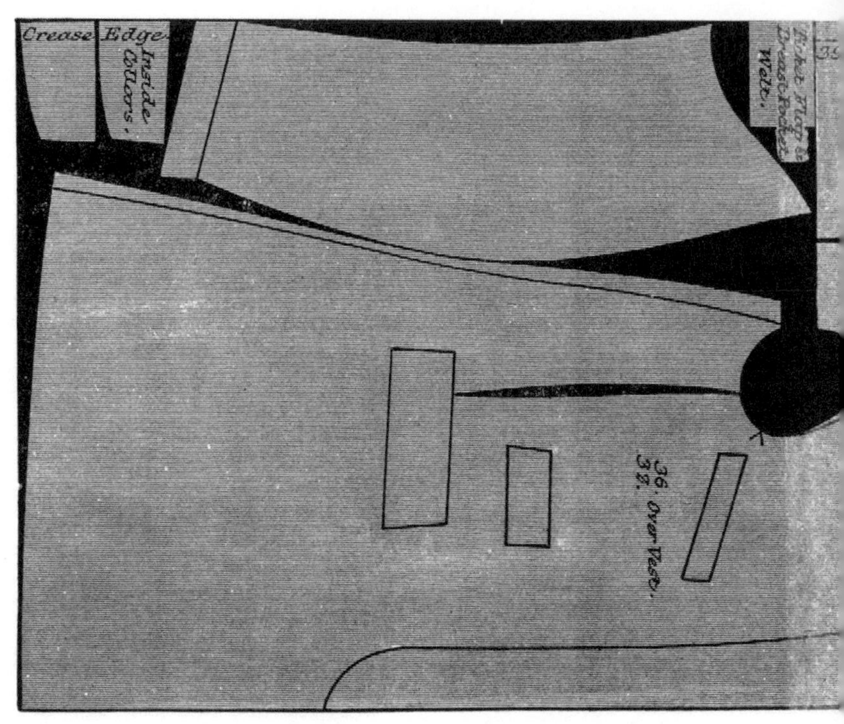
Crease Edge.
Inside Collars.
Ticket Flap & Breast Pocket Welt.
36. Over Vest. 38.

Cape Facings.
Shoulder Facings.
Crease Edge.
Inside Collars.
Facings.
Ticket & B.P. Flaps.
38. Over Vest. 34.

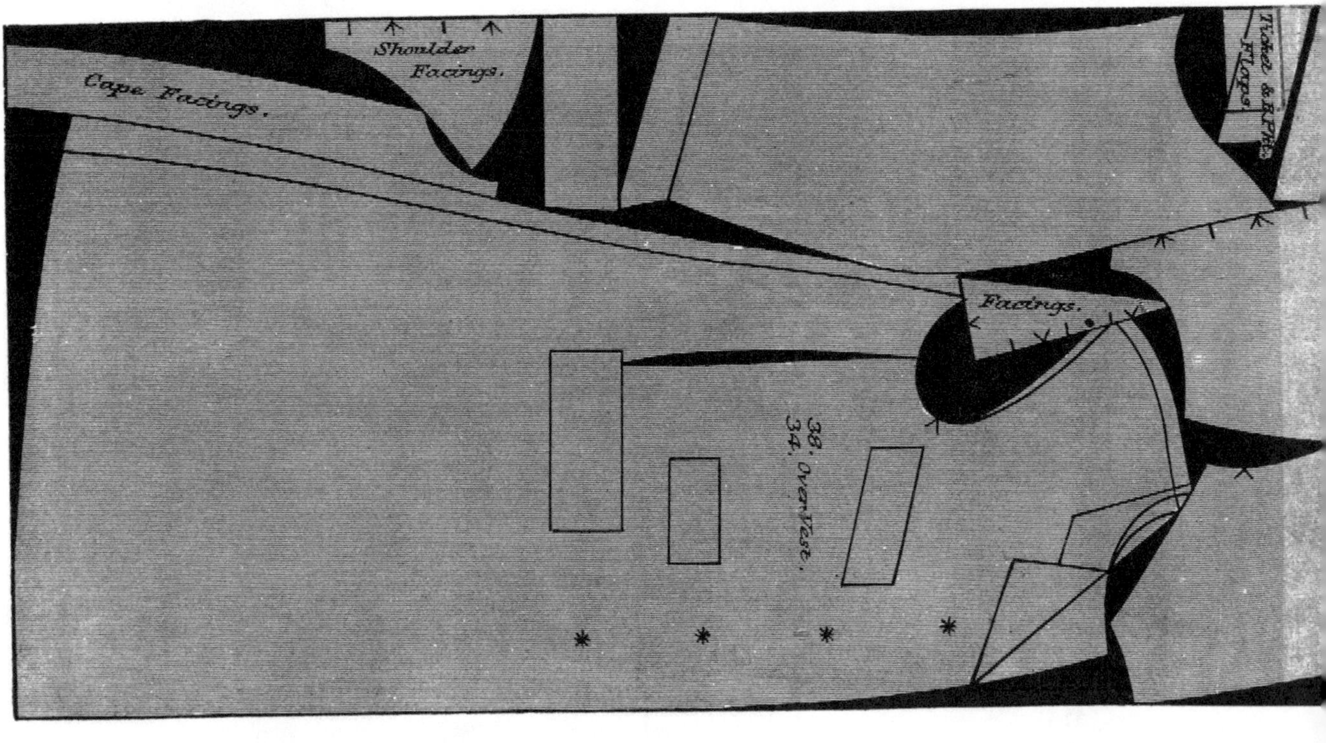

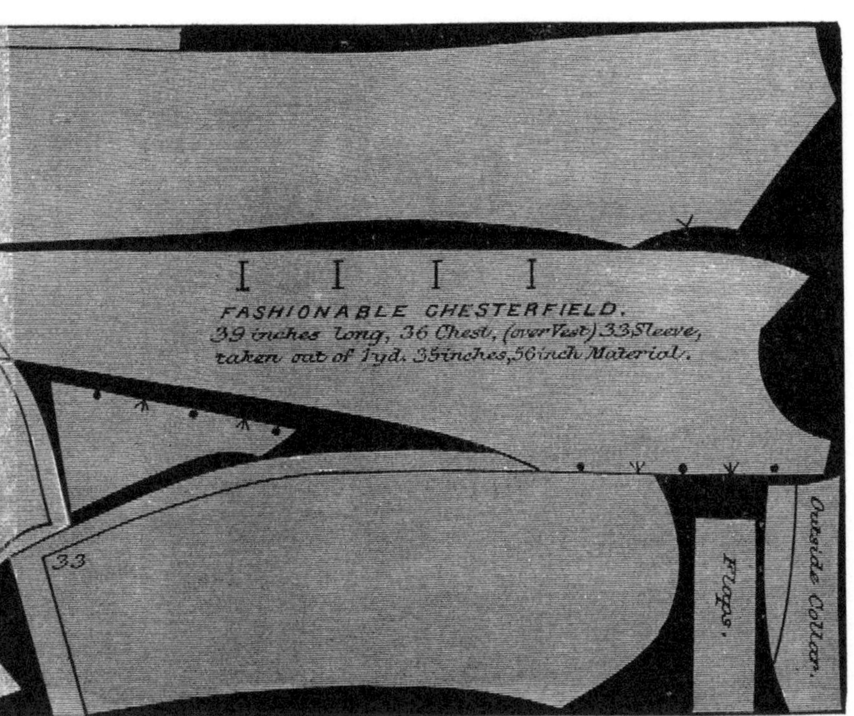

FASHIONABLE CHESTERFIELD.
39 inches long, 36 Chest, (over Vest) 33 Sleeve,
taken out of 1 yd. 35 inches, 56 inch Material.
33
Flaps.
Outside Collar.

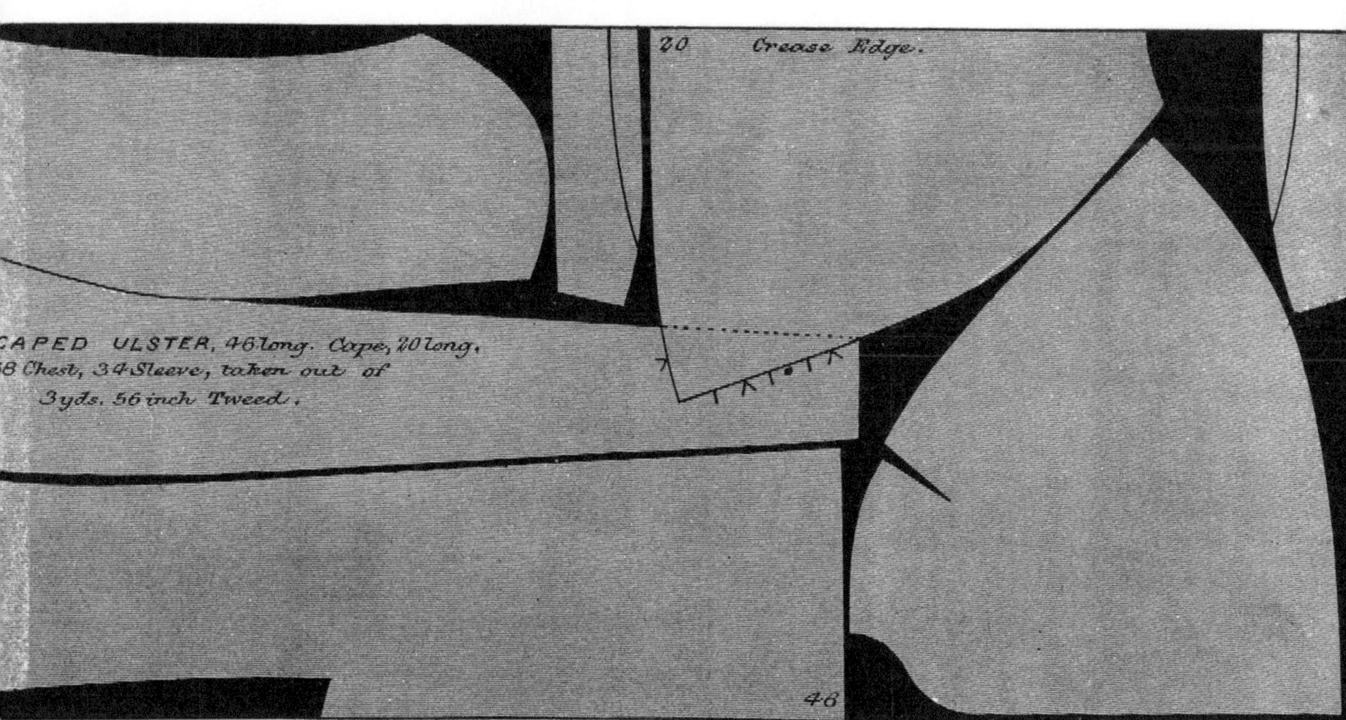

20
Crease Edge.
CAPED ULSTER, 46 long. Cape, 20 long,
48 Chest, 34 Sleeve, taken out of
3 yds. 56 inch Tweed.
46

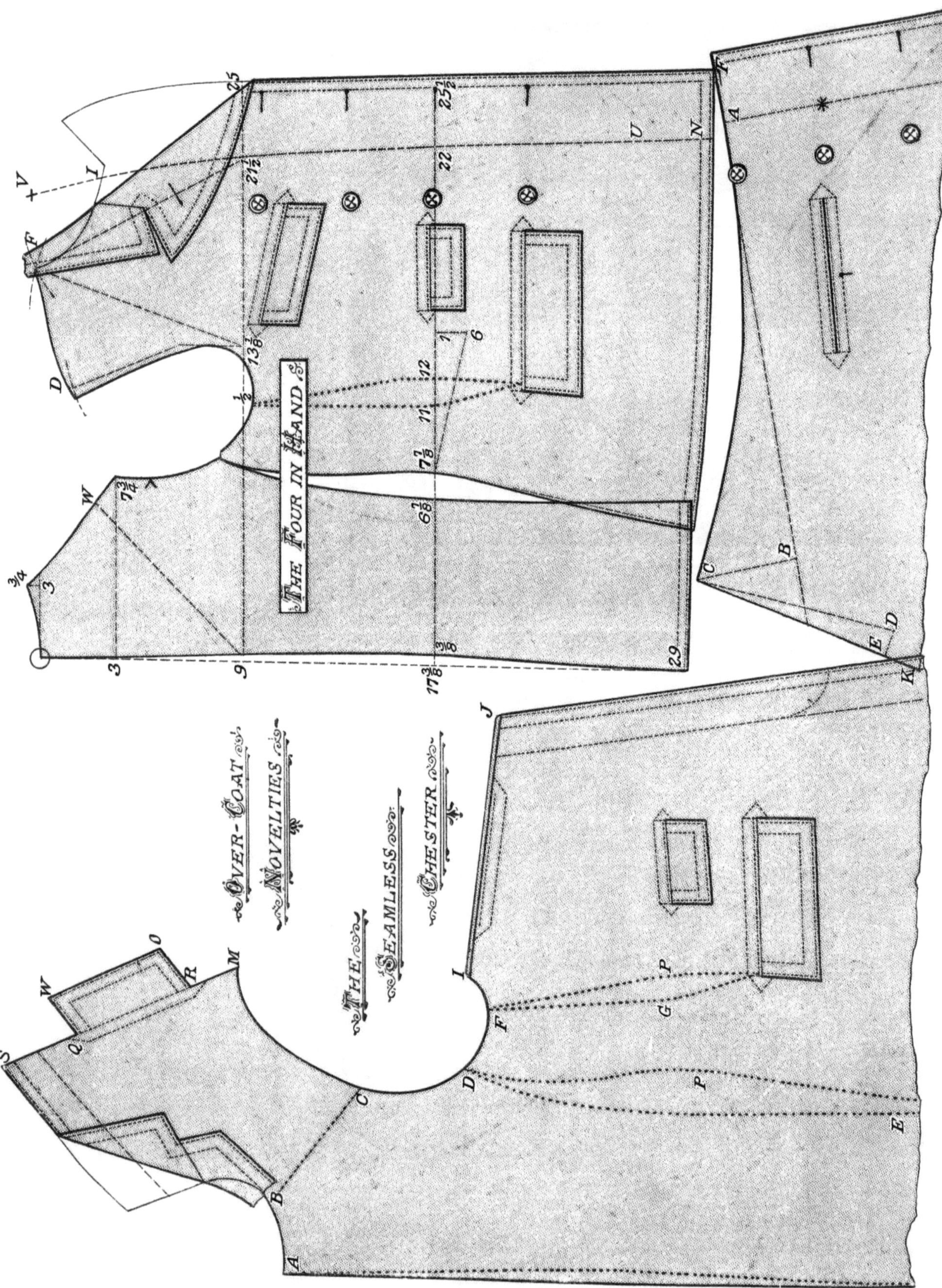
THE FOUR IN HAND.
OVER-COAT
NOVELTIES
THE
SEAMLESS
CHESTER

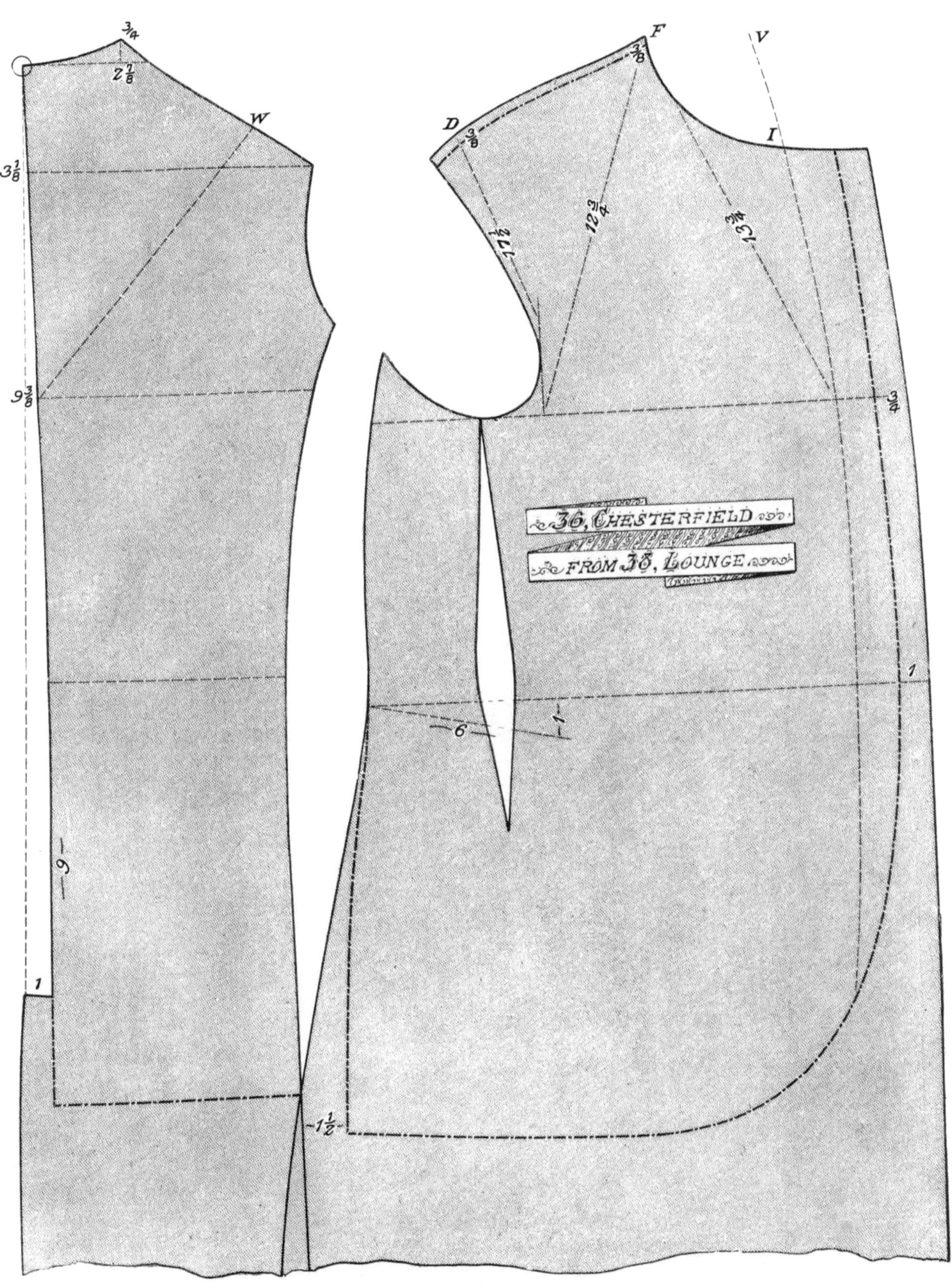
3/4
Z 7/8
W
F
3/8
V
D
3/8
I
3 1/8
7 1/2
12 3/4
3 3/4
13
9 3/8
3/8
36, CHESTERFIELD
FROM 38, LOUNGE
1
9
1
6
1
1 1/2

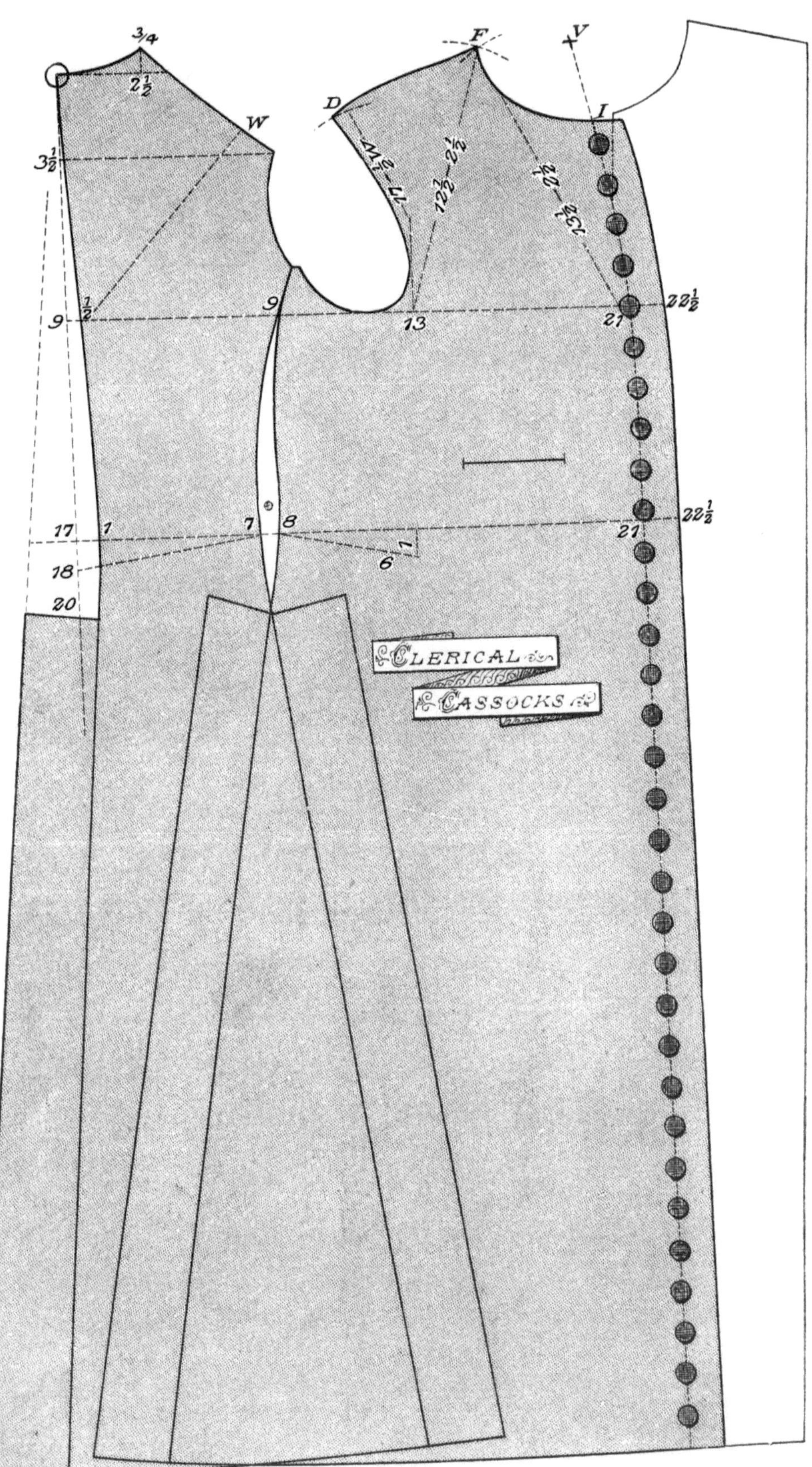

3/4
2½
3½
½
9
17 1
18
20
W
9
13
D
12½ 2½
22½
7 8
6 1
21 22½
21 22½
F
V
I
13½ 2½
2½
Clerical
Cassocks

LIST OF PATTERNS.

TROUSERS:

Fashionable Models, smart and clean fitting, cut in the present style.

Waist	31	82	33	34	35	36	37	38	39	40	41	42	43	44	45	46	47	48	49	50
Seat	36	38	39	40	40½	41	41½	42	42½	43	43½	44	44½	45	45½	46	47	48	49	50

Also the following which are cut 30 to 42 waist, varying 2 inches a size.

WORKING MEN'S WHOLE FALLS, very easy fitting.

BELL BOTTOM TROUSERS, smart fitting fronts close-fitting knee and large bottoms.

WEST END MODELS, as cut by a leading West End specialist.

THE CITY TROUSERS, wonderfully successful, a good cut for smart trade.

RIDING TROUSERS, narrow legs, and specially cut for riding purposes.

BREECHES, GAITERS, &c.

All cut 30 to 42 waist, varying 2 inches a size, unless otherwise stated.

HUNTING PANTALOONS, as cut by the most fashionable trades in the West End. Very full at thighs, clean fitting at leg seam. continuations cut on.

RIDING BREECHES, as worn by most gentlemen. Full in thighs, close-fitting at knee, sideseam well to front at knee. Useful set. Fly fronts and specially suited for use in the saddle.

FARMERS' BREECHES, the seat and thighs have about same ease as trousers. Sideseam comes well to front knee.

LIVERY BREECHES, very close-fitting at thigh and knee, fair amount of ease at fork. Buttons well forward at knee. These embody all the well known characteristics of Livery Breeches.

INFANTRY KNICKER BREECHES. The well-known military design, the best style of garment for walking or riding.

KNICKERS, suitable for walking, cycling, &c., may either be finished with elastic or knee band, medium size in body, fair width in legs.

RACING SHORTS, Bathing Drawers and under drawers, cut in the most approved style for each garment.

LITTLE BOYS' SHORT TROUSERS, 20 to 26 waist, varying 2 inches.

YOUTHS' FULL LENGTH TROUSERS, 24 to 30 waist, varying 1 inch a size.

LADIES' EQUESTRIENNE TROUSERS, 20 to 28 waist, varying 2 inches.

LADIES' EQUESTRIENNE BREECHES, 20 to 28 waist, varying 2 inches.

LADIES' CYCLING KNICKERS, 20 to 28 waist, varying 2 ins

LADIES' BLOOMER KNICKERS, 20 to 28 waist, varying 2 ins.

BISHOP'S GAITERS, Livery Gaiters, Gentlemen's Leggings, Gamekeeper's Leggings, all cut 13½, 14, 14½, 15, 15½.

SPATS to fit over boots 6, 7, 8, 9, 10.

CHILDRENS' GAITERS to fit boys of 3, 4, 5, 6, and 7.

LADIES' GAITERS, 13½, 14, 14½, 15. 15½ calf.

PUTTEES of military regulation, width and length.

VESTS.

31 to 50 breast, unless otherwise stated.

S.B. No-Collar Vest ; S.B. Step Collar Vest ; S.B. Dress Vest ; Footman's Roll Collar Dress Vest ; Sleeve Vest, S.B. or D.B. ; Dress Vest Horseshoe Opening ; Clerical Stand Collar Vest ; Clerical Dress Vest ; Clerical Cassock Vest ; Bishop's Apron ; D.B. New Style Vest, hollow crease row, buttoning high.

LADIES' VESTS, S.B. stand collar, 28 to 40 breast.

LITTLE BOY'S VESTS, button to throat, 22 to 26 breast.

YOUTH'S VESTS, S.B. No-collar, 26 to 30 breast.

COATS, JACKETS, &c.,

31 to 50 breast, unless otherwise stated.

FASHIONABLE LOUNGE whole back and forward fronts.

LARGE SHOULDERED LOUNGES (Muscular Men's Models) smart in fit, easy in scye, and specially suited for provincial trades.

FASHIONABLE REEFERS cut in smart style (or from Muscular Men's Models) the D.B. fronts and lapels thoroughly up-to-date cut with whole backs.

THE NORFOLK JACKET, pleats cut on, a very easy fitting garment, pleat up each front and back.

THE NORFOLK JACKET, pleats to sew on, an easy fitting smart garment.

DRESS JACKET with roll collar and rounded fronts, a very smart and stylish jacket.

DRESS JACKETS with pointed lapel and forward front, as now made in leading West End trades.

WAITERS' JACKETS, a short semi-dress Jacket for waiters, ship stewards, &c.

MORNING COATS, smart fitting (or from Muscular Men's Models) moderately cut away, moderate length.

THE SHOOTING COAT, forward skirts, rather short easy scye and forward cut sleeves.

D.B. FROCK COAT, intended to button 3, lapels and front cut in West End style, very useful set.

OPEN FRONTED FROCK COAT, specially designed to fit closely when worn unbuttoned, excellent set for spring and summer trade.

THE "THREE M's" from the celebrated Muscular Men's Models specially suited for well developed men, who require provision for ease and comfort combined with smart style and fit,

LIVERY FROCK as worn by coachmen, S.B. and specially designed to meet requirements of that class, 32 to 44 breast, varying 2 inches.

ROLL COLLAR DRESS COAT, cut in harmony with latest fashion, very smart and stylish.

POINTED LAPEL DRESS COAT, cut in the style now adopted by leading West End firms.

FOOTMAN'S COATEE, especially cut to embody the special features of British Liveries.

GROOM'S FROCK, exceedingly smart.

PAGE'S JACKET, close fitting body garment.

FLY FRONT CHESTERFIED, three seam back and fit moderately close.

FLY FRONT CHESTERFIED with whole back, sac fitting, new coat for 1904.

D.B. CHESTERFIELD, with whole back and easy style of fit.

FLY FRONT RAGLAN, easy fitting, sleeve, V on the shoulder.

ALSO YOKED RAGLAN, 31 to 50 breast varying, 1 inch.

D.B. ULSTER AND CAPE, easy fitting with moderately full cape, designed for travelling purposes.

THE SCARBORO' OVERGARMENT cut without sleeves, moderately full cape.

INVERNESS COAT, with narrow back and shaped shoulder.

OLD STYLE INVERNESS CLOAK with wide back full cape.

LIVERY OVERCOAT, suitable for coachmen or footmen.

The John Williamson Company Limited. 42, Gerrard Street, Shaftesbury Avenue, London, W.

SPECIALITIES.

Fireman's Tunic. D.B. front as worn by the Metropolitan Fire Brigade, 34 to 46 breast, varying 2 inches.

Police Tunics as worn by the Metropolitan Police Force, 36 to 48 breast, varying 2 inches.

Butchers' Frocks, 34 to 48 breast, varying 2 inches.

Duck Jackets, as worn by workmen, 34 to 46 bt. varying 2 ins.

Engineer's Combinations, Trousers and Coat in one, 34 to 46 breast, varying 2 inches.

Patterns for the Wholesale Trade.

We are prepared to undertake to design special sets of patterns as required for the wholesale trade, sets graded by our special method. This ensures absolute correctness for all sizes, particulars of price and sizes on receipt of directions for order.

HOSIERY PATTERNS.

Pyjama Suits, S B. Jackets, and Trousers without sideseam, with or without feet, 32 to 44 breast, varying 2 inches.

Flannel Shirt Pattern with turn back collar included, 32 to 44 breast, varing 2 inches.

White Skirt Pattern, 32 to 44 breast, varying 2 inches.

Night Shirts, 32 to 44 breast, varying 2 inches.

Dressing Gowns with D.B. fronts and roll collar, 32 to 44 breast, varying 2 inches.

Smoking Jackets, B.B. fronts. roll collar, rounded fronts 32 to 44 breast. varying 2 inches.

JUVENILES.

Eton Jacket, 24 to 30 breast, varying 2 inches.

Norfolk Jacket for little boys, 22 to 30 breast, varying 2 inches.

Boy's Lounge, collar and turn, 22 to 30 breast, varying 2 inches

Round Jacket, fastening up to front, 22 to 28 breast, varying 2 inches.

Sailor Jacket, 22 to 28 breast, varying 2 inches.

Jack Tar Blouse, 22 to 28 breast, varying 2 inches.

Highland Doublets, 22 to 28 breast, varying 2 inches.

Spanish Blouse, with cape collar, 22 to 28 breast, varying 2 inches.

Boy's Dress Jacket, 26 to 30 breast, varying 2 inches.

Fly Front Overcoat, 24 to 30 breast, varying 2 inches.

Little Boy's Overcoat, to be worn over skirt. 22 to 30 breast, varying 2 inches.

Fry Front Covert Coat, 22 to 30 breast, varying 2 inches.

Inverness Cape, 22 to 30 breast, varying 2 inches.

D.B. Ulster with Cape, 24 to 30 breast, varying 2 inches.

MILITARY.

Universal Service Frock, 34 to 46 breast, varying 2 inches.

" " " D.B. Frock Coat, 34 to 46 bt., varying 2 inches.

Tunic, 34 to 46 breast, varying 2 inches.

Doublet, 34 to 46 breast, varying 2 inches.

Lancer's Tunic, 34 to 46 breast, varying 2 inches.

Patrol Jacket, 34 to 46 breast, varying 2 inches.

Cavalry Overcoat, 34 to 46 breast, varying 2 inches.

Infantry Overcoat, 34 to 46 breast, varying 2 inches.

United Service Mess Jacket, 34 to 46 breast, varying 2 inches.

" " Mess Vest, 34 to 46 breast, varying 2 inches.

Infantry Trousers, 34 to 46 waist, varying 2 inches.

Cavalry Trousers, 30 to 42 waist, varying 2 inches.

Cavalry Pantaloons, 30 to 42 waist, varying 2 inches.

CLERICAL.

Library Jackets, 34 to 46 breast, varying 2 inches.

S.B. Frock Coats, 34 to 46 breast, varying 2 inches.

Clerical Dress Coats, 34 to 46 breast, varying 2 inches.

" Inverness Cape, 34 to 46 breast. varying 2 inches.

Long Surplice, 34 to 46 breast, varying 2 inches.

Short Surplice, 34 to 46 breast, varying 2 inches.

Pulpit Robe, 34 to 46 breast, varying 2 inches.

M.A. Gown, Oxford, 34 to 46 breast, varying 2 inches.

B.A. Gown, " 34 to 46 breast, varying 2 inches.

M.A. Hood. B.A. Hood. Oxford or Cambridge.

S.B. Cassock, 34 to 46 breast, varying 2 inches.

D.B. Cassock, 34 to 46 breast, varying 2 inches,

S.B. Vest. 34 to 46 breast, varying 2 inches.

Cassock Vest, 34 to 46 breast, varying 2 inches.

These Models will be added to from time to time, as fresh styles are introduced. We are always prepared to cut patterns of any styles of garments that customers may require.

The John Williamson Company Limited. 42, Gerrard Street, London, W.